THE FACE
BEHIND THE MASK

SHATTERING THE SECRETS
THAT KEEP YOU STUCK

DELEISHA L. WEBB

DEDICATION

This book is for the adult who has gone through life wearing "the Mask." The Mask that hides insecurities, shame, and secrets. The Mask that hides depression and anxiety. The Mask that hides the "real you." The Mask that allows you to be a mother, a father, a loving spouse, a sister, or a brother, and a professional. I wore my Mask far too long. As my Mask began to shatter, the "real me" started to shine through. The "real me" was broken and hurt. It was my ex-husband who knew the "real me." It was my ex-husband who really pushed me to start this journey of writing.

This book is dedicated to my ex-husband, Ronnie Darrell Smith. As my intimate partner, Ronnie experienced many of My Truths. My Struggles. My Secrets. My Insecurities. He encouraged me to share my story, hoping it would help other people who have shared my experiences. Ronnie inspired me to help others understand the direct and indirect realities of growing up with a drug-addicted parent. His support pushed me to share my love and passion for working with my neglected and abused babies. He motivated me to share my struggles as well as my many triumphs in helping children and families. Ronnie thought it was important that I allow others a look into my life as a social worker.

Or, as he used to say all the time, "The life of a social worker." Because he was my husband, he also experienced the advocacy, the crisis responses, the mentorship, and the education that I provided to my students and families. Ronnie had a very giving spirit and a big heart. He helped many of my children and families in the time of crisis. Ronnie's support and understanding of my personal struggles got me through many, many hard times. Throughout our fifteen-year relationship–nine years married and six years of friendship after the divorce, Ronnie has given me the strength, encouragement, and support to share my story with others.

Thank You, Ronnie Smith!

While I was writing this book, Ronnie lost his life due to complications from the coronavirus. He was admitted into the hospital for pneumonia and covid related issues. The Lord called him home on Feb. 2, 2021. Ronnie will always and forever be in my heart.

#RIH Ronnie Darrell Smith

#SmithStrong

TABLE OF CONTENTS

FOREWORD

"From the struggles of her soft and tender childhood years and into adulthood, Deleisha balances sacrificial love and beauty with the erratic ugliness of addiction. Peering through her childhood eyes, you can almost feel her attempts to desperately grab hold of all the good while persisting through adversity as her heroes at times disappeared to fight their own demons. As a young parent, Deleisha pens what it means to balance harsh reality with forgiveness while intentionally appreciating moments of laughter and loyalty in between. From family diseases to family healing, to your own personal healing, you will gain an intimate insight into recovery and unconditional love through it all. This book will take you on a journey through a young woman's life who has lived through and overcome pain, succeeded and fallen, been broken and yet called, rebuilt, and renewed, compelling you to come face-to-face with what's behind your own mask."

Enjoy the journey of "The Face Behind the Mask."

Stacey McDonald, Ed. S.

PART 1
THE MASK

INTRODUCTION

Despite the challenges I have had in my life–childhood sexual abuse, parental substance abuse, emotional/mental abuse, mental health issues, and teenage parenting, I found the strength and determination to push through and overcome those barriers. When I think back over my life and ALL that I have been through, I thank GOD for blessing me! My daily testimony! Although I dealt with those obstacles, I have never considered my life dysfunctional until my therapist pointed out that I live in dysfunction. In my third session with her, I sat on her brown leather couch with one knee bent under me. I was feeling nervous and anxious because she was asking me questions I was not ready to answer. I sat and cried in silence as she began writing on her chalkboard. The first word she wrote was "DADDY," and it was big and loud. Just seeing the word made my body tense up. I could feel and hear my heart pounding loudly. *Why is she asking me about my Daddy? I wasn't here to talk about my Daddy. I came to talk about my divorce.*

I had reached out to my therapist on my forty-fourth birthday. I felt as if I was having a total mental breakdown on the day that I should have been rejoicing. I took the day off from work and spent the day alone. I had attempted to get my driver's license changed back to my maiden name. This was my third visit to the DMV, and after being told that I didn't have the correct documents, I broke down in tears in the DMV lobby. *What is happening here? Why can't I get my license changed? Why do I have to get my license changed? I didn't want my marriage to end in divorce.* My heart was breaking at the fact that I needed to change the name on my license. I did not want a divorce, but...it was too late. I was divorced. The clerk took me to her cubicle and allowed me to make the changes without the appropriate documents. She witnessed that I was in a fragile state and just needed to get it done.

After leaving the DMV with my name changed back to my maiden name, I drove straight to Lake Norman. I needed to be alone to process my feelings and emotions. With tears in my eyes, I sat at a picnic table looking at the ducks. The sun was glistening on the lake. In the distance was a mother with two toddler-aged kids playing in the sand. My emotions overtook me, and I cried uncontrollably. I didn't know the specific reason why I was crying, but I couldn't stop the flow of tears. I was struggling with the truth. I was a forty-four-year-old divorced woman. I hadn't wanted the divorce. With the proper help, my marriage could have been saved. But the reality is that I was the one who filed for divorce. Both my ex-husband's and my pride got in the way of our love and commitment to one another. The fact was I didn't know how to manage and process all of those emotions while actively engaging in a "fling" with my ex-husband.

Those are the reasons I was here to see my therapist, not to discuss my Daddy.

My therapist turned around to me, and as she took a seat in her black leather recliner, she said, "Tell me about him." She pointed at the word on the board. I looked at the word and said it aloud to myself, "my Daddy."

"Yes, your Daddy. Tell me about him," she repeated.

I sat back and let my back melt into the couch as I thought about my Daddy. How do I describe him? What words can honestly describe my Daddy? My Daddy–He is an AWESOME Daddy, AWESOME Friend, a Double AWESOME Granddaddy, and a Double AWESOME Great-Granddaddy. At the age of sixty-seven, my Daddy is one of the coolest, down-to-earth, funniest, most handsome, and helpful men I know. That is how I described him to my therapist. I am a Daddy's Girl. My Daddy is also selfish, a manipulator, a liar, and an addict. Yes, addict! My Daddy is addicted to drugs–Crack Cocaine, I think. I do not know his drug of choice because I have never seen him use drugs. I have never seen him under the influence of drugs that I can remember. Even then, I did not know he was "high" until he told me he was "high." On that day, he apologized to me for seeing him under the influence. I couldn't even look at him. I didn't want to look at him, knowing that he was "high." I drove him to his destination, let him out of the car, and drove off without looking back. Tears rolled quietly down my face as I drove home.

CHAPTER 1

WHO AM I?

Here is the million-dollar question, "Deleisha, why are you here?" My therapist looked me square in the eyes as she put down her Bible. My therapist considers herself a Christian woman and often references scriptures in the Bible. She is a Licensed Professional Counselor and a Christian Life Coach. I have made the comment that I "*need to get my life together.*" I was working with my therapist to do just that. One would think that my life is quite good. Why is that, you ask? Well, let me tell you about the Mask that I wear.

I finished high school with honors. I went straight to college and earned my associate degree in Business Management from Lexington Community College. I attended the University of Kentucky and earned my Bachelor's Degree in Family Studies. I became pregnant during my first semester in college. Later, my son was born. I was only out of college the semester I gave birth. Then, I returned to school and completed my degree.

My son's father committed a crime when I was six months pregnant. He participated in a robbery at Taco Bell that resulted in a man being shot and killed. He was charged with Robbery and Reckless Homicide. When my son was just six months old, his father was sentenced to ten years in prison. I raised my son with the help of my immediate family and his dad's immediate family. My mother and my son's paternal grandmother were key in his upbringing. While I was in school full-time and working part-time, the grandmothers helped me care for my son. After finishing my bachelor's degree, I worked full-time for two years before deciding to go back to school to earn my Master's in Social Work. While in graduate school, I continued to work. Again, my family was there to support and assist me. My mother and my son's paternal family provided the assistance I needed to accomplish my educational goals while working to support my son.

Is single parenting hard? Yes. Is raising a son without a father around hard? Yes. Was any part of this single parenting easy? Absolutely not. Nonetheless, with the right support, it was manageable. To most people, my friends, and my family, my life was easy. My life presented with no struggles or issues. I had three degrees. I had a good job, and I made decent money. I had been on my own since my son was six months old. My bills were paid. My son had everything he needed and most of what he wanted. He was active in sports (which was expensive).

My immediate family, which includes my mom, dad, and my sister, is very close-knit. We do everything together. We have a ton of family traditions! To everyone on the outside, my life was good. A good life with no dysfunction or issues is what my Mask represented. My Mask looked good on the outside. I was cute. I had my own place. I had nice clothes. I had a good job. I had a nice car. I had an extremely supportive family. However, what people did not know is that I was suffering from many insecurities, pains, struggles, anger, sadness, guilt, and shame behind the Mask.

Many times, my dad said that my life is perfect. He would say, "You have a good job. You make good money. You have a good husband who loves you (when I was married). You do whatever you want to do. You go wherever you want to go. You buy whatever you want to buy. Your life is good, Deleisha." I cannot recall how many times my dad has said that to me. Little does he know that everything he named that I had or have does not exempt me from feeling sad, anger, fear, pain, guilt, anxiety, or shame. However, one would never know it because of the Mask. The Mask looks good on me, and I wear it well. However, there is a whole lot of "stuff" behind that Mask. Let me start with the first man that I loved, my Daddy.

My dad is one of my best friends. He is the coolest, dopest, funniest, craziest, most awesome man that I know. He is an EXCELLENT grandfather and an EXCELLENT great-grandfather. He is an EXCELLENT dad. However, in the midst of his excellence, he is a drug addict. I grew up with a drug-addicted dad. He has been a drug addict for most of my life. Nevertheless, he is the "Bomb Addict." Again, one would never know that my dad is a drug addict because of the Mask.

CHAPTER 2

THE ADDICTION

Why Do Fools Fall in Love

My first memory of learning that "something" was going on with my dad was when I was around six years old. Although his behavior was very bizarre and scary, I did not know that it was related to drug use. My mom was in the kitchen cooking one of her favorite meals for dinner– pork chops with instant mashed potatoes. She still had on her white nursing dress and white, soft sole shoes. My dad walked into the kitchen and put five one-hundred-dollar bills on the kitchen table. My mom immediately turned around, picked up the five one-hundred-dollar bills, folded them up, and put them inside her bra. I was sitting on the couch watching one of my favorite cartoons, "Tom and Jerry," when I witnessed this exchange. Then, I watched as my Daddy went into the bathroom. I waited patiently for him to come back out to play with me. Our usual routine was for my dad to sit next to me and ask how my day was. He would always say, "How was school today, Dee?"

I always answered with a big smile. "My day was good, Daddy. Today we played outside on the playground, and then I fell when I was running back inside," laughing at the thought, although I was embarrassed when it happened in front of my friends.

"Why were you running, Dee? Were you playing catch?"

"No, Daddy. I just like to run, Daddy. You know how fast I am. I can beat you running too," I would giggle and take off running through the apartment. My dad would let me get in the hallway before he got up to catch me. I would go running into my bedroom and hide in the tiny closet. I would hide in my usual hiding space, which was behind my big brown teddy bear. The teddy bear used to be in the corner of my bedroom but was eventually moved to the closet because its shadow would scare me.

"I'm coming to get you!" My dad would yell. He would pretend not to know where I was hiding, although I always hid in the same spot in the closet. I would hear him open and close the bathroom door saying, "You're not in the bathroom. Where can you be?" Then I would hear him go into my parents' bedroom and look in the closet. "She's not in my closet. Pat, where is Deleisha hiding?" My mom would ignore him and just laugh at our game. Finally, I would hear his footsteps coming into my bedroom. I would squeal at the anticipation that my Daddy was getting ready to find me.

"Here I am, Daddy!" I would scream and jump out of the closet. "You can find me, Daddy!" I had the biggest grin on my face. My face always lit up at my Daddy. One thing was and still is for sure–I am a Daddy's girl. I always felt comfort, protection, and peace when my dad was home. He was my hero. To me, my Daddy was the toughest, strongest, funniest man on this earth. That was my typical day. I always looked forward to my Daddy coming home from work so we could play.

However, this day was different. My dad seemed to be preoccupied. He was not thinking about playing with his little girl. He was in a hurry to leave back out of the house. After placing the money on the kitchen table, he kissed me on the cheek and went right back out the front door. I sat on the couch, waiting for him to come back inside to play with me. But he did not come back, not at that time, anyway. He did not come back until I was in bed. It was after 8:00 p.m. I know because my bedtime was at 8:00 p.m. I had been lying in bed trying to go to sleep for about thirty minutes when I heard the locks turning on the front door. From my bed, I could see my mom sitting on the couch in her light, pink gown. She had her right leg crossed and was swinging it as she chewed on her Double Mint gum. I know it was Double Mint because I used to sneak into her purse and steal pieces of gum. I chuckled at the thought. Yea, I was a little sneaky at times.

After a few minutes, I could hear my dad yelling, "Give me the money, Pat!" The loud boom of my dad's voice made me shiver. It scared me to hear my Daddy yell because that signified that he was truly mad. Although his voice made me shiver, I walked out into the hallway to see what was going on. I looked from my dad to my mom.

My mom responded with a soft cry. Her face remained free from tears, but the sound of her voice was crying out, "No, Buster, it's the rent money. The money is for the rent, and I have to pay the rent tomorrow." Buster is my dad's nickname. Everyone in my family called him by his nickname. They continued to argue over the money. Both of their voices were loud, and their loudness made me cry. My dad became frustrated and got up to start looking for the money in their bedroom. As I stood in the hallway, I saw my dad go through the drawers in the nightstand and throw the contents on the floor. Then, he pulled all the drawers out of the dresser and threw the clothes on the floor. My dad attempted to stuff the clothes back in the drawers in an unorganized fashion. When he did not find the money, he began to run his hands under the mattress. Becoming more and more out of control, he took the mattress off the bed and peered under it. He looked in the closet, in all of the hiding spaces he could think of. By this time, he was getting more and more destructive and violent as he continued to look for the money.

My Mother was hysterical and asked my dad to leave the house. I could tell she was crying by the way her voice cracked when she spoke. Afraid and not understanding what was happening, I continued to stand in the hallway listening to my parents argue. As my dad continued to scream at my mother, he became scarier and scarier by the minute. I had never seen my dad act that way before. My little six-year-old body continued to stand there in shock as I watched the scene unfold.

With tears in her eyes, my mother yelled, "Leisha, go call your Granny! Now!"

I picked up the phone. My six-year-old hands were shaking. I was scared. I had never heard my parents yell at each other this way. My hands were shaking so badly that it took me a few times to dial the number on the rotary phone correctly. My mother's cries got louder. She yelled for my dad to get out of the house. I called my Granny and told her what was happening. She could hear them arguing through the phone. My Granny told me to go to my room and said she was on her way. I never went to my room.

Granny arrived at our house within fifteen minutes. She came inside and yelled, "What's going on in here?"

My mom explained to my Granny that my Daddy was trying to take the rent money back. She explained that my dad was tearing up the house looking for the money he had given her earlier.

Granny told my mom, "Give me the rent money." My mother gave Granny the rent money. Granny took it, folded the bills, and placed them in her bra. She looked at my dad and told him to leave the house right now. I can remember my dad looking pitiful and embarrassed. His facial expression resembled the look a little boy in my classroom would make whenever he got in trouble. It was a look that I'll never forget. My Daddy put his head down in shame and walked out of the front door. He dared not argue or talk back to his mother. My dad had not said one word since she came into the house. My Granny did not play. She said exactly what she meant and meant exactly what she said. I had never seen anyone disrespect my Granny. After my dad left, my Granny asked my mom for the rest of the rent money and told my mom that she would pay the rent tomorrow morning. After giving me a big hug and a kiss, she walked me to my room. Granny said a bedtime prayer with me and tucked me in bed. She helped my mom clean up the bedroom, and then she left.

I can remember still feeling scared and anxious after my Granny left. I was scared my dad would come back and demand the money again. I stayed awake for most of the night. My mom allowed me to sleep in the bed with her because she knew I was scared. My six-year-old mind thought my mom was probably afraid my dad would come back, too. Cuddled up next to my mommy, I eventually fell asleep.

The next day, I woke up, and everything was back to normal. My dad was sleeping in my parent's bed. My mom was cooking breakfast. Everything was normal. My parents never discussed the situation with me. No one told me that my dad had a drug problem during that time. However, I had overheard many conversations that my mom had with her mother, her sisters, and her sister-in-law, my dad's sister. Those conversations always included the words "Buster" and "drugs." I heard my mom tell my Granny that my dad wanted the money for drugs. Although I was just six years old, I heard enough to know that my dad was using drugs. I just did not know what "drugs" were or what drugs he was using.

When I think about that day now, it reminds me of the movie, *Why Do Fools Fall in Love*. The movie is about Frankie Lymon, a singer who died of a heroin overdose. In the movie, there is a scene where Frankie came home and demanded money from his wife so he could go out and continue to get high. She refused to give him money, telling him that it was for the bills. After destroying the house looking for the money, he held her puppy out the window as a threat to make her give him the money. She eventually gave him the money, but he accidentally dropped the puppy out the window. Whenever I watch that scene, it reminds me of the time I had to call my Granny on my Daddy. Even after that day, my Daddy was still the Bomb Daddy. My Daddy. I am a Daddy's Girl.

Family Vacations

I grew up in Lexington, Kentucky, known as the Horse Capital of the World. Every summer, our family vacation consisted of a three-day trip to Ohio. My Daddy, my mom, my sister, and I would leave on a Thursday and return home on Sunday. On the one-and-a-half-hour drive to Cincinnati, Ohio, my Daddy would always get lost. Whenever we went out of town, my Daddy's role was to drive, and he always made it comical. Although we made the exact same trip every summer, my Daddy would never drive us directly to the location. We always ended up making wrong turns or on the wrong highway. In true Daddy-fashion, he would never ask for help with directions. He would drive until we made it to our destination.

On the drive, our family would sing songs and play games. My favorite games were "I See Something that you Do Not See" and "Punch Buggy." No matter the game, my Daddy would cheat all the time. It makes me laugh every time I think about it. He was funny like that. My Daddy would also tell funny stories about my sister and me. We would laugh at every single word he said.

Although my mom has always been on the quiet side, she participated in the fun and games too, always playing and laughing with us. Her smile was everything! She was so happy when we were on vacation as a family. My parents would get a suite, so there was plenty of room for my sister and me to run around and play. My sister and I are seven years apart; I'm the oldest. Even with our age difference, we played well together. It was fun being a big sister. It was not until my teenage years that the sibling rivalry started. It was the typical big sister–little sister relationship. Everything I did wrong, she told our parents. She was a tattletale, even as we got older. I would pay her to keep my secrets, but she still told on me. Tattletale.

We always went to Kings Island, an amusement park in Mason, Ohio, during our weekend vacation. My family has always been roller-coaster fanatics. We would ride every roller-coaster that I was big enough to ride. When my sister came along, we spent a lot of time in the Kiddie Park so she could enjoy the park as well. My parents would get on every ride with us. As my sister got older, we all rode on the roller coasters. We are a Roller Coaster family. My parents would buy us whatever we wanted at the amusement park. We got every toy and/or souvenir we wanted. My family would spend the entire day at the amusement park. We arrived when the gates opened and stayed until dark to see the beautiful display of dazzling fireworks, which signified the park's closing.

We would spend an entire day at the Cincinnati Zoo. My dad's favorite zoo exhibit is the Gorilla Den. My dad always pretended the gorillas were talking to our family. He would pretend to have conversations with them and said he knew their secret language. My mom played right along with my Daddy. Because of the interactive times we had and the way my dad made it seem so real, the Gorilla Den became my favorite exhibit as well.

To this day, it is still my favorite exhibit at any zoo. My family always had a great time at the Cincinnati Zoo.

Once the Waterpark opened in 1985, we would spend half a day at The Beach Waterpark across from Kings Island in Mason, Ohio. Both of my parents enjoyed getting into the water. My dad would splash around in the wave pool, getting my sister, my mom, and I soaked from head to toe. My dad and sister would get on the water slides that were appropriate for my sister's age. I did not enjoy the water slides because I didn't like my head going under the water. Therefore, my mom and I would lounge around in the lazy river. My dad always brought water guns into the water park so we could have a water gunfight. My mom seemed to "bow out gracefully" because she did not want her hair wet. After all, she kept her hair styled and pretty. I wanted to be just like her.

Our family vacations were important to my parents and were so much fun. They made sure we had a family summer vacation—a weekend away before returning to a new school year, even if they did not have the extra money to go. A few times, my dad did not go with us when he "blew his money" on drugs. On those rare occasions, it was just the three of us–my mommy, my sister, and me. Although it was weird not having my dad with us, we had a great time. We still played games and sang songs on the ride to Ohio. We never got lost when my mom drove. My mom made sure we had just as fun, even in my dad's absence. Even when my dad did not join us on vacation, he was still the Bomb Daddy.

Stolen Goods

NIKE. I absolutely love Nike shoes and clothing. I started working at Long John Silvers, my first job, the day after my sixteenth birthday. I worked there for over a year. Every paycheck, I bought myself a new pair of Nike Air Max tennis shoes and/or Nike clothing. Red, black, and white are my favorite colors. I remember buying myself a red, black, and white Nike sweatsuit. I fell in love with the sweatsuit when I saw it at Lazarus, now called Macy's. I saved my money to buy the sweatsuit to go with my new red, black, and white Nike Air Max tennis shoes.

It was a Friday evening, and I was getting my clothes ready for my Saturday outing with friends. I was so excited to finally wear my new sweatsuit and matching Air Max tennis shoes. As I was looking through my closet, something did not feel right. I could not find my sweatsuit. I looked at every piece of clothing in my closet. I carefully looked from left to right, then right to left. It's not here! I cannot find my sweatsuit. I went to my parents' bedroom and asked my mom if she had seen my sweatsuit.

"No, Leisha. I haven't seen it," mom said.

"Has it been in your closet at all?"

She shook her head, "No, Leisha."

As I walked into my bedroom, I began to cry silently. The more I cried, the angrier I became. In my heart, I knew my dad had taken my sweatsuit and sold it. It wasn't the first time he had violated my property that way. I'm so angry at him. *How dare he steal my clothes that I bought with my own hard-earned money and sell them.* My hands became sweaty at the thought of me confronting my dad. Although I was angry and disappointed, he was still my daddy. I eventually cried myself to sleep.

Later that evening, I heard the door open, and my dad walked in. I confronted him, "Daddy, have you seen my sweatsuit?" My voice was frantic and almost sounded shrill.

Daddy immediately denied seeing my sweatsuit. "No, I haven't seen it. Why are you asking me?" he said with a defensive tone. He dismissed me and walked into the kitchen.

At first, I was shocked by his non-emotional response. Quickly my shock turned into anger. *Why are you being defensive?* There was no reason for him to get defensive, especially if he had nothing to do with my sweatsuit. After a few days, I started fearing that my dad did have something to do with my missing sweatsuit. His response and lack of emotion hurt me. I was thinking to myself, *"What did I do to you?"* You're the one who has stolen from me, your child! Just as quickly as my anger grew for my dad, I became angry with my mother. I could not understand why she was okay being with a man who has and continues to steal from his family. I took my anger to my bedroom, slammed the door, and wrote in my diary. I couldn't wait until I turned eighteen so I could move out of the house.

About a week later, my dad asked me to sit down so he could talk to me. With his head down, he explained, "I took your sweatsuit to my friend, Don's house, with the intention of wearing it. But I never wore it because it was too small. So, I left it at his house. After hearing his explanation, I knew it wasn't true. I knew he was telling me a lie just to break the tension between us. I was speechless because he was telling a flat-out lie, and he was bringing his best friend into his lie. I had nothing to say. I looked at him, acknowledged his comment, and walked away.

The next day, I went to Don's house to get my sweatsuit. I pulled in front of his apartment window and honked my horn. Don would always come to the window, if he was home. He raised the screen up as I got out of my car. I walked to the window and said, "Hey Don, my dad said he left my sweatsuit over here. It's a red, black, and white Nike sweatsuit. Can I get it?"

Don did not look me in my eyes as he said shamefully, "I don't know where your sweatsuit is, Leisha. I will look for it, though. Come back in a few days."

I went back the next day and every day after that for about a week. Finally, Don told me the truth, "Your Daddy did not bring a sweatsuit to my house. I'm so sorry, Leisha," he said looking disappointed.

Before I left, I looked at my Daddy's best friend with tears in my eyes and thanked him for being honest. I knew the story didn't make sense because my dad could not fit my clothes. But, because I wore my sweats slightly bigger than my normal size, it wasn't far-fetched for my dad to put on my hoodies or jackets.

Eventually, my dad admitted that he took my sweatsuit and sold it. Like a kid caught stealing, he put his head down because he couldn't look me in the eyes. "I'm so sorry, Deleisha. I'll give you $100 when I get paid next week." When I didn't respond, he stood up and walked away like a wounded puppy. I don't know what he expected me to say to him. What was I supposed to say to my Daddy who just admitted that he actually stole from me? I had never felt such agony and affliction. It was like a gut punch in my heart. He never paid me back. Nevertheless, he was still my Daddy.

Imagine being seventeen years old and working hard and saving money to get an outfit that you really want. Then when you have saved enough money, you go to the mall and buy that outfit. As a teenager, you are filled with pride as you purchase your outfit with your own hard-earned money. Then imagine you never get to wear it. Take it one step further. You have to accept the fact that your own dad stole your outfit and sold it to feed his drug addiction. Can you imagine the pain I felt? Although I knew he had sold my sweatsuit, it still hurt. I was disappointed and shocked that my own dad would steal from me so he could get drugs. I felt so let down by him. MY Daddy. He stole from his firstborn child. His baby girl. As with anything, in time, I learned to forgive him. Until it happened again...

In July 1993, I turned eighteen years old—I was legally an adult but still a child living at home with my parents. I had finished high school in May and was working part-time until school started in August. I will be attending the University of Kentucky in the fall. One night, I came home from work and went straight to my bedroom. I was exhausted. I had worked a double shift that day because someone called in at the last minute, and I wanted to be a team player. After taking a shower and putting on my pajamas, I walked into the kitchen to warm up my food. As I walked past my dresser, I noticed that I did not see my necklace and rings, which were usually sitting on the corner of my dresser. Although it was weird, I did not give it much thought that night because I was tired and needed to get ready for bed.

The next morning, I had plans to hang out with my boyfriend, my high school sweetheart of two years. I got dressed in some cute jeans and a white T-shirt. After combing my hair, I went to put on my jewelry. Again, I did not see my necklace or rings. I had a cute 14-karate gold necklace with a heart pendant that my boyfriend had bought for me. I also had four gold rings. Obviously, nothing expensive at that age, but nonetheless, they were nice for a teenager. I looked on my dresser. No necklace or rings. I looked in my dresser drawer. No necklace or rings. I looked behind my dresser. No necklace or rings. My heart began to beat fast. Tears stung my eyes as I tried not to immediately accuse my dad. However, in my heart, I knew that my dad was responsible for my missing jewelry. Even though it was not worth more than $500 total, it was still mine. My mom wasn't home, so I called her on the phone and asked if she had seen my necklace and rings. She had not. I decided that I would confront my dad about it when I got back home. My boyfriend picked me up, and we enjoyed the day together.

Later that evening, when I returned home, I walked into an empty house. No one was home. I went straight to the kitchen to get a snack. Passing through the living room, I noticed that the VCR was not on top of the floor model television. *Maybe the VCR in my parents' room is broken, and they took the one from the living room.* I walked into my parents' room, and the VCR from their room was missing as well. Wow, both VCRs are missing! Reluctantly, my mind went to wondering again. My Daddy. Then I remembered that my jewelry was missing this morning. Something is not right. Before I could call my mom to inquire about the missing VCRs, she walked in the front door.

"Mom, what happened to the VCRs?" I looked at her, waiting for an answer. She did not respond right away. I looked at her and noticed she had tears in her eyes. Again, I asked, "Why are the VCRs missing?"

Without looking at me, she responded, "Your dad sold them." Without saying another word, my mom walked past me and went directly into her bedroom. She looked exhausted, weary, and defeated. It broke my spirit to see my mom like this. My mom was always in a happy mood. She rarely appeared upset or mad. On those rare occasions, her emotions were a direct result of my dad's drug-addicted behaviors.

I walked to her bedroom door and said, "Mom, I think Daddy took my necklace and rings. I have looked all over my bedroom, and I can't find them anywhere," my voice was in an elevated tone. I was angry but not at my mom. I did not know if it was because of my tone or her anger, but my mom did not respond to my comment. She completely ignored me. Her lack of response made me even more upset. With tears running down my face, I ran into my bedroom and slammed the door behind me. Curled up in my bed, I called my boyfriend and vented to him about my dad and his drug problem. He comforted me, and we talked on the phone until we fell asleep.

I awoke the next morning to the smell of bacon. The smell of bacon was always a good sign that my mom was in a good mood. Putting on my robe, I walked into the kitchen and saw my mother sitting at the round glass table with a plate in front of her. She greeted me, "*Good morning, Leisha!* Fix your plate." I grabbed a plate from the counter and filled it up with eggs, bacon, and toast. As I sat at the table, I looked at my mom. She appeared much happier. She told me she wanted to talk with me.

"Deleisha, your dad will no longer be living here. I cannot put up with his behaviors anymore. He has stolen money from me. He has sold or pawned our electronics. Your dad has a drug problem, and he needs help."

I continued to eat my food as if I did not just hear those things about my Daddy. *I am a Daddy's Girl.* It hurt me to listen to those things about my dad. However, I knew all of that. My dad had been stealing my mom's money and pawning electronics for years. Let us not forget that he sold my NIKE Sweatsuit the year before. Moreover, he never paid me back for it either.

My mom continued talking, in between taking bites of her food. "He pawned your jewelry. I will replace it next month." My mother was always paying my dad's debts. A look of relief overcame her after she disclosed that my dad would be leaving the house. I had mixed emotions about what I had just heard from my mom. Of course, I did not want my dad to leave the house. However, I understood my mom's frustration and anger. A few days later, my dad apologized again and said he would pay me back. Of course, he did not. My Daddy. *I am a Daddy's Girl.*

Holiday Traditions

Holidays are a "big" event for my family. My maternal and paternal sides of my family celebrate the main holidays in a big way. Both of my parents come from large families. My mother is the oldest of eight kids. My dad is the second oldest of nine kids. Although my extended families had traditions, we had our own family traditions. Christmas has always been my favorite holiday tradition of them all. Around four weeks before Christmas, we would go as a family to pick out a real Christmas tree. We would decorate the tree together and sing Christmas songs and tell stories. My parents would wrap most of our gifts and have them under the Christmas tree. On Christmas Eve, my parents would help us bake chocolate cookies to leave for Santa Claus, along with a glass of milk.

After watching a good Christmas movie and playing a few games, my parents would make us go to bed, saying that Santa Claus will not come to our house until we were asleep. I can remember being so excited about Santa Claus that I could hardly fall asleep. My sister would go straight to sleep because I would threaten her. I would tell her that Santa Claus would put pepper in her eyes if she were not asleep when he got to our house. Once my parents thought we were fast asleep, I could hear them bringing out the big toys. Those were the toys that were too big to wrap or required assembly. I could hear them dragging the boxes from their hiding places through the hallway. They would be up talking and laughing while getting the living room prepared for Christmas morning.

Christmas morning was so exciting. I would usually be the first one up. I would shake my sister and tell her to go wake up our parents. Once they were out of bed, my sister and I would go running into the living room to see what Santa Claus had brought us for Christmas. We would spend the morning opening gifts and playing with our toys. Those were some great times! We had plenty of good times and still do!

Present Time

Christmas remains a big deal for our family. We all spend Christmas Eve and Christmas Day together. We gather at my sister's house and have a sleepover. Our Christmas Eve activities consist of games, movies, and our annual talent show. We all participate in the talent show—my boys, my husband (at the time), my mom, my dad, my sister, my nieces, and my sister's husband. I often wonder how this tradition will change if either of my parents were to remarry. We allow the kids to open one gift on Christmas Eve. The adults pick the gift the kids are allowed to open. After the talent show and family movie, we send the kids to bed so Santa Claus can come.

On Christmas Day, we all open gifts together. We let the kids open all their gifts before the adults open their presents. The love my immediate family has is one to be treasured. I feel so blessed to have this type of bond with my immediate family. I have been Blessed to *never* experience a Christmas without my mommy. I am forty-five years old, and I can count on one hand how many Christmases I have had without my Daddy. Those few times were due to his "getting high" and not wanting to expose the family to his "after usage" looks. My Daddy. *I am a Daddy's Girl.* I am Blessed. We are a Blessed Family.

The Piggy Bank

I was twenty-one years old with a two-year-old son, Joel. I was living on my own in a two-bedroom apartment. I participated in a program called Virginia Place–One Parent Facility, now called One Parent Scholar House. It is a housing program for single parents who are continuing their education beyond high school. I was attending the University of Kentucky, working on my bachelor's degree. It was a summer weekend, and I had planned to go to the beach for a quick getaway with some friends. My dad asked if he could stay at my apartment and babysit Joel for the weekend while I was gone. At that time, he had gained some of my trust back. He had not been getting high or going on drug binges that I was aware of. Because of that, I was feeling more comfortable with him being around. *I am a Daddy's Girl.*

My son **LOVED** his granddaddy. I left my dad with my son in my apartment along with my car for the two days I would be away at the beach. I had constant communication with him on Friday and during the day on Saturday. By Saturday evening, I could no longer reach my dad. I called my mom and asked if she had heard from my dad, but she had not. She started calling around and found out that my son was at my Granny's house, my dad's mom. I called Granny, and she told me that my dad asked her to watch Joel for the night. My dad had dropped Joel off at her house a few hours earlier. I thanked her for watching him.

After knowing that my son was safe with my Granny, I was able to enjoy my last night at the beach with my friends.

When I returned the following evening, my car was parked in front of my apartment complex with the keys under the front seat. There was a note left in the driver's seat that simply said, "I'm sorry." I shook my head and threw the note on the ground. I was sick of hearing those words, "*I'm sorry.*" After going into my apartment, my anger seared. My dad had busted open my son's blue crayon piggy bank and had stolen *all* the money inside it. It was all the money that my son had been given since his birth. There must have been at least $500 in that piggy bank. A few days later, I discovered my dad apparently found my new alternator in the trunk of my car with the receipt stuck inside the box. He told me that he took my car to my uncle to get the new alternator put on my car. So, I assumed my car had at least been repaired. Nope. He had taken the new car part back to the store and gotten a refund. My dad got me yet again. My Daddy. *I am a Daddy's Girl.*

#1 Fan

My son started playing sports when he was four years old. What sport can kids play at the age of four? T-Ball. Joel and my little cousin signed up for T-Ball and played on the same team. The very first game was hilarious! Imagine a team of four-and five-year-old kids playing T-Ball for the first time. My little cousin walked up to the batter's mound and hit the ball off the tee. Then she just stood there and smiled—a big smile. She was the cutest, smiling girl on the team. She never ran the bases. She just smiled! Joel was up next. Of course, I was cheesing from ear to ear. I am super excited for my little cousin and my son. Joel hit the ball, ran, and picked up the ball, and then took off running the bases with the ball in his hand. Absolutely hilarious! We laughed so hard at the kids playing!

"Go, Joel!" My dad yelled out to the field. "Run, Joel, run!" My dad literally ran the bases with Joel, even though Joel was still running with the ball. My dad was so excited to see Joel play T-ball. He would often be at the T-ball field before I made it up there! That very first game was the beginning of my dad following around his #1 player–his grandson!

Basketball came next for Joel. For the next two years, Joel played basketball and baseball. When he turned seven, he added football to his plate. As he got older, baseball became his favorite sport. He began playing for an American Amateur Union (AAU) Baseball Team. Joel played for the Southside Bulldogs for about four years. Guess who was at every single game and many of the practices? You guessed it...my Daddy! A lot of the times, my dad would ride with us to Joel's practices, scrimmages, and games. On those days that I did not pick my dad up because he would already be at the field or court when we arrived. We did a lot of traveling with this team. Guess who traveled with us? If he could not make the games, guess who called every hour on the hour to get an update on the games? My Daddy. Joel's granddaddy. Joel's coach. He was his #1 Fan!

Joel played sports from age four until he graduated from high school–baseball, football, basketball, and track. He played sports for his middle and high schools as well as outside AAU Traveling Leagues. Talk about a busy kid. Guess who was there for EVERY SINGLE GAME/TRACK MEET? You guessed it again... my Daddy. Joel's granddaddy.

My Daddy was not just there for sports; he has been there for every milestone in Joel's life, big and small. Joel's first crawl. Joel's first steps. Joel's first words. First day of preschool. First day of elementary. First day of middle school. First day of high school. Every awards ceremony and celebration in Joel's classes. Every birthday. High school graduation. Moving Joel into his college dorms at St. Augustine University and Lenoir Rhyne University. Joel's first apartment and subsequent apartments. My Daddy. Joel's granddaddy. He has NOT missed a single moment when it comes to his role as Granddaddy. He is the Bomb Granddaddy.

Ruining Vegas

By this time, my father had been doing well in his recovery. I had no knowledge of him using any drugs or getting high in several, several, several months. Because of this, I started to trust him again. I became more and more comfortable with him being at my house, around my purse around, any money laying around, and watching my son. My fiancé and I decided to take a few days and go to Vegas. Our boys, Joel and Matt, my stepson, requested that granddaddy watch them for those days. They loved their granddaddy and always want to spend time with him. Again, he is an EXCELLENT granddaddy. After discussing it with the family, we decided to ask my dad to watch the boys. He agreed. The plan was for him to watch the boys at our house. We left for Vegas on Thursday morning. *We left $100 for the boys to do whatever my dad wanted to do with them. We left the car with a full tank of gas. We left plenty of food in the fridge.* I checked in with my dad and the boys a few times on Thursday evening. Once I felt confident that everything was okay, I stopped calling. On Friday morning, I spoke to my dad several times. He told me the plan for the day was to pick the boys up from the bus stop, take them to eat pizza, and then go to a movie. He also planned to pick up my mom, so they could all hang out for the evening.

Later that afternoon, I started calling my dad–no answer. I called the home phone, my dad's cell phone, as well as the boys' cell phones–no answer. I called my mom–no answer. After about two hours of calling, I began to panic. I was all the way in Las Vegas and had no idea where my boys were or what was going on at my house. I could not focus or enjoy myself because I was a nervous wreck. I kept praying that my boys were safe and not in harm's way. Several hours later, I finally spoke to my mom. She said she had not heard from my dad. I asked her to go to my house and see if the boys were there. She did. However, no one answered the door, and my car was not in the driveway. I asked my mom to sit there and wait. She did.

About an hour later, my mom called me. She told me the boys had just come back to the house. Joel had a key to get into the house–it was 7:00 p.m. I spoke to the boys and asked if they were okay. They said they were fine. They had been outside playing basketball over a friend's house. I asked them if they knew where their granddaddy was. They told me that granddaddy went to get pizza several hours ago and never came back. The boys were having so much fun outside they didn't notice how much time had passed. At that point, I knew my dad was **MIA** (*Missing in Action*). I asked my mom to look through the house to see if anything was missing. I asked her to look in my bedroom, in my closet, to see if my jar was still there. We had a large jar filled with money—bills and coins. My mom did not see the jar in the closet. She said everything else looked okay in our bedroom. However, nothing was okay. I was just relieved that my boys were safe, and my mom was there to stay with them.

Can I tell you how I was feeling? I was all the way in Las Vegas, and I could not enjoy myself because my children had been left home alone AND my dad was MIA with my car! All I could think about was what if something had happened to my boys! My boys had been outside playing for hours, and my dad was nowhere in sight. *How heartless can he be? How inconsiderate can he be?* I could not believe my dad's indifferent attitude towards the suffering of his family. Thank God my boys were safe! Thank God that I was finally able to reach my mother and have her go to my house. My mother stayed with the boys for the remainder of our trip. My dad showed up at the house late Sunday evening. He called my mom and let her know the car was in the driveway. He asked her to meet him at the door to give her the keys. He didn't want to go inside the house or have the boys see him because he was ashamed and embarrassed, as he should have been!

My fiancé and I came home to find the gas tank in my car was completely empty. There was mud and dirt all over the outside of the car. The $100 we left for the boys was gone. The jar that was always kept in our closet was found hidden behind the window curtains and was completely empty of all the bills, but the change was still in the jar. There were about $520 in bills that we had counted before we left for Vegas. Needless to say, I did not hear from my dad until two days after we got home. Initially, I would not take his phone calls. After he called about five times, I decided to answer. He asked if we could meet to talk. *What do we have to talk about? What is there to say? Another, "I'm sorry"? I'm sorry gets old after hearing it your entire life.* But he's my Daddy, so I eventually agreed to meet with him. Can you guess how that conversation went? After his same old apology, I thanked my dad for bringing my past into my present. He would always say that those "drug behaviors" were in the past. I thanked him for reminding me of who he really is–an addict. I thanked him for completely spoiling our Vegas trip. I thanked him for thinking only of himself and completely disregarding the safety of his grandsons.

What more could I have said? How would you have responded to your dad? What would you have said? Would you have called the police and made a police report? Would you have reported your car stolen over the weekend? I thought about calling the police on him. I threatened to call the police on him and report my car stolen. I thought about pressing criminal charges against him and getting the Department of Social Services involved because he had left my boys home alone. I thought about many things. How do you respond to something like this? We all react differently to traumas and crises in our lives. I could never have imagined that I would ever consider calling the police on my dad. While I was beyond angry for a long time, I eventually forgave him, but I will *never* forget. After all, he is my Daddy. *I am a Daddy's Girl.*

In my adulthood, I have learned that my dad's drug of choice is cocaine. Cocaine. The disclosure came out during a family therapy session when my dad was in treatment. My dad has been to several treatment facilities over the years. He has been to detox, inpatient, and outpatient treatments. He has had some success in his recovery. The longest I can remember him remaining clean is about a year. One thing I have learned during this addiction process is addiction is for a lifetime. There will be relapses. I never knew very little about Cocaine until I became an adult. Now let me educate you on what I've learned about Cocaine.

According to drugabuse.gov, here are some interesting facts about Cocaine:

South Americans have chewed and ingested coca leaves which is the source of cocaine, for their stimulant effects.

In the early 1900s, purified cocaine was the main active ingredient in many tonics, and elixirs developed to treat a wide variety of illnesses and was even an ingredient in the early formulations of Coca-Cola.

Before the development of synthetic local anesthetic, surgeons used cocaine to block pain.

This is the information that is most common to us:

Cocaine, also known as the "caviar of street drugs," is a high-priced way of getting high. Cocaine has extremely negative effects on the heart, brain, and emotional wellbeing of users. Many users become physically and psychologically dependent upon the drug, which can lead to long-term and devastating life-threatening consequences.

Cocaine is a Schedule II drug, which means that it has a high potential for abuse but can be administered by a doctor for legitimate medical uses such as surgeries.

Cocaine is a recreational drug that is created by purifying an extract from the leaves of the coca bush. Different processes produce the two primary forms of cocaine we see on the street. Powdered cocaine...is often snorted but is easily soluble in water and can be injected. Crack cocaine, or "crack" or "rock" on the streets, is created using a chemical process that produces a freebase form of cocaine that is smoked. The immediate effects or the high produced by cocaine usually wear off between thirty minutes and two hours after use. Smoking or injecting coke leads to a faster, yet shorter high than snorting the drug.

I first heard about cocaine in middle school through the DARE Program. After completing the program, I vowed I would never use drugs. Not weed and definitely not cocaine. While I have experimented with weed use, I have never tried cocaine. At that time, I never could have imagined that I would come to have such a strong, intimate relationship with cocaine. Sounds funny to say I have a relationship with a drug that I have never used. Well, I do. How do I have a relationship with cocaine? Let me tell you. Addiction is a family disease. When one family member struggles with addiction, the entire family is affected. The disease of addiction puts all family members in a state of heightened stress and anxiety.

According to the American Addiction Centers, "Feelings of guilt, responsibility, confusion, anger, sadness, and more can trouble the entire family and lead to increased conflict, isolation, and dysfunction." Every household member in my family experienced these feelings. Not just my immediate household members, but some extended family members experienced it as well.

In response to my dad's drug addiction, I have developed some unhealthy patterns. Unhealthy communication, misdirected anger, misguided expectations, self-medicating, and ignoring are some of the patterns that have plagued me.

The American Addiction Centers speak about unhealthy patterns:

As family members attempt to control the addictive behaviors and cope with the condition, many new patterns form. If your family member is struggling with addiction, you may begin to form some unhealthy patterns, including:

- Negativity in communication. With many complaints and criticism, your communication can be harsh and encourage conflict in relationships.

Many times, I was negative and harsh in my communication. I didn't recognize that I was displaying negativity and harshness, but looking back today, my tone and presentation were definitely negative.

- Misguided expectations. Your beliefs about and expectations of your loved one and their condition may be off-base and cause you to be perpetually disappointed.

Expectations of my dad were most times off-base. Although I know that drug addiction is an illness, it's an illness that's hard to accept as being unintentional. In the past, and even today, I struggle with the idea that my dad would do something to cause me harm. Then I have to remember that his behaviors are those of an addict and not a "normal" person.

- Misdirected anger. Feelings about your loved one's addiction may be inappropriately expressed towards others.

Anger. I find myself angry for no reason. Over the years, my family members, immediate and extended, have referred to me as "the mean one," and it used to hurt my feelings. Even strangers would approach me and say, "Smile, pretty girl. You're too pretty to look so mean." After some self-reflection, I realize that I have displayed a mean spirit over the years. The way I spoke sounded mean. The way I responded to people seemed mean. My demeanor was unpleasant and unfriendly. I have never been rude or disrespectful, just unapproachable. That meanness and unhealthy communication had become one of my main coping mechanisms.

- Self-medication. You, yourself, may eventually use substances to manage the stress that is growing from the family member's addiction.

Over the years, I have struggled with depression and anxiety. I have been prescribed medication to help with my mood. It became easy to Mask my pain with medication. Although prescribed by a medical doctor, taking medications can be considered self-medicating if the prescription instructions are not followed.

- You may attempt to cope or keep the peace by ignoring all warning signs and acting as if nothing is wrong.

Another coping mechanism has been for me to ignore the problem. I do not ask my dad any questions about his addiction. I do not confront him when he "messes up" or goes on a drug "binge" for days at a time. I do not confront him when he misses an important family event. I do not address the addiction at all. I never thought about it as ignoring the problem, but ignoring it helped me to cope.

Those descriptions are word-for-word what I have and continue to experience while coping with my dad's addiction. Most people would not know it or understand it. Thus, the Mask I Wear. Although these coping mechanisms appear to work, I have learned in counseling that they are unhealthy ways to cope. I have also developed two of the most severe unhealthy patterns, codependency and enabling.

Look what American Addiction Centers say about Codependency and Enabling:

Two of the more serious maladaptive interactive patterns to develop in the face of family addiction are codependency and enabling.

- **Codependency**-The state of being <u>overly concerned with the family member</u> while spending little time and energy on your own needs. Codependent family members may:

  o Have low self-esteem.

  o Appear very controlling because they do not trust their family member.

  o Seem overly flexible to avoid anger and rejection.

  o Have oversensitive reactions to problems.

  o Stay loyal and dependent on the person no matter what.

  o **Enabling**-The state of constantly working to protect the family member from the natural consequences of substance use. By making excuses, bailing their loved one out of jail, paying for legal fees, and otherwise staving off negative consequences, an enabler prevents the family member from experiencing the true cost of their addiction firsthand.

Children are not immune to changing family dynamics. In many situations, roles reverse, and the child begins to take on the caregiving role for their substance-abusing parent. This can create extreme stress for the child, blur the appropriate boundaries, and set the child up for difficulty setting healthy boundaries in future relationships.

Codependency and enabling are challenging behaviors to identify within yourself. I had trained my mind to believe my actions were helping my dad. Not so true. My behaviors and the behaviors of many of my family members have been harmful to my dad. For many years, I believed my dad would not get high if I made sure to talk to him on payday. If I picked him up from work and spent the day with him, he would not get high. *If I did this* or *if I did that*, then my dad wouldn't get high. It took me a long time to realize I was taking on ownership of his addiction. Codependency.

The first time I sought out counseling to address my feelings towards my Daddy, my therapist gave me a book to read, *Codependent No More*. She recognized that I had taken complete ownership of my dad's addiction, and it was affecting me negatively. Because I was so concerned with making sure my dad didn't get high, I ignored my own needs–mentally and emotionally. I had done things I didn't want to do. All in the name of *saving* my dad from getting high. Instead of helping my dad, I was hurting myself. I have stolen food for my dad. I made excuse after excuse for him when he had done something to hurt Joel. I provided financial assistance to my dad after he had gotten high and could not pay his bills or buy food. I denied his addiction. I have ignored his addiction. Codependent and enabling behaviors, you name them, I did it. Again, all in the name of *saving* my dad from getting high. Although my dad is at the core of this issue, I don't blame him. He was behaving like an addict. My Codependency is a "me" issue that I continue to address today. My Daddy. I am a Daddy's Girl.

My codependency and enabling behaviors have spilled over into other relationships. My therapist recently told me that I am showing signs of codependency with my son. My life focus has been my son. I have always felt like I needed to intervene to stop him from being hurt, from hurting anyone else, and from suffering real-life consequences. Like my dad, I have made excuses for my son. I just wanted to keep them safe and unharmed. In my self-work, I recognize that not allowing them to have natural consequences is harming them. Without consequences, behaviors seldom change. One must be held accountable to learn from their actions. I told my therapist about my history of codependency with my dad. "Ahhh, that makes sense," she responded. Yes, it all made sense. I had developed this codependent and enabling relationship with my dad as a young child, and it carried over into my adult relationship with him.

THE FACE BEHIND THE MASK

Adulthood Daddy

Throughout my life, my dad and I have had many challenges. Some good. Some bad. Some ugly. We are a lot alike. I can remember we had a horrible argument that almost turned physical, and I told him, "I'm just like you. I am a chip off the old block. The only difference is, I don't use drugs, and I don't steal from my kids and grandkids!" I remember spitting that venom at him in anger. The look on his face turned from complete shock to shame. He looked like he wanted to cry out in shame and punch me at the same time. I did not care. I wanted to hurt him. I wanted him to know how much he had hurt me. You know the saying, *hurt people who hurt you.* It took us a long time to recover from that altercation. It took me many, many months to forgive him for the comments made during that altercation.

Nevertheless, I will *never* forget. I have not forgotten all the heartaches and pains caused by my dad's drug addiction. However, I do understand that his actions are the actions of a drug-addicted man. It took me a while to understand his behaviors and not take them personally. After many years of reading about and attending Narcotics Anonymous Meetings, being educated in Family Studies and Social Work, and through life experiences, I am much more educated about the life of addiction. Because of this knowledge, I am able to love my dad unconditionally.

I have spent many, many years in counseling to address my "Daddy issues." Once I came to terms with my "Daddy issues," I became able to focus on "my own issues" and appreciate all of my challenges with my Daddy. Despite it all, my Daddy has been there. My Daddy. *I am a Daddy's Girl.*

My Daddy has been there with me through every milestone in my life. I do not remember a birthday without my Daddy. He was there for all of my graduations–from elementary school, middle school, and high school. My Daddy was there when I found out I was pregnant with my son. He was the person who gave me "the talk" and let me know that I was loved and supported no matter what. My Daddy was there for the birth of my son. I cried for my Daddy to be in the room when I delivered Joel, but he could not do it. I understood. My Daddy was there when I graduated from Lexington Community College with my associate degree. He was present for my graduations from the University of Kentucky-Undergraduate and Graduate School Graduations. I do not remember a time when I moved that my Daddy did not help me. He helped me pack, clean, physically move my furniture, and unpack–including when I moved from Kentucky to North Carolina. My dad walked me down the aisle while singing to me when I got married. (Mind you, he had gotten high a few days before, so I was concerned if he would show up). My Daddy was there when my bonus son came into my life. He accepted and loved him as if Matt was his biological grandson. My Daddy was there when my ex-husband and I separated. He was there when my divorce was final. My Daddy was there when my grandchildren were born. Guess what? He has not missed a milestone in either of their lives.

My dad has even been by my side through this entire process of self-work and self-discovery. He does not understand why I have the feelings and emotions that I struggle with, but he supports me through the process. My Daddy supports my dreams and aspirations. He supports my writing this book as part of my healing. He doesn't feel good about it, but he supports me, nonetheless. Over the last year, I have had some medical issues. My Daddy has been there for every one of my medical procedures. He has taken me to my appointments and sat in the car for hours because no one could accompany me due to COVID-19 restrictions. He stayed with me while I was recovering and catered to my every need. Even when I am not sick, my Daddy caters to my every need. Any food that I crave, my Daddy will come to my house and cook. My dad has always been there for me! My Daddy. I am a Daddy's Girl.

Now, here I am, forty-five years old. I am still a *Daddy's Girl.* Is my Daddy perfect? Not by a long shot. Am I perfect? Are any of us perfect? Not by a long shot. Nonetheless, my Daddy is as *perfect* a Daddy, Granddaddy, and Great-Granddaddy as one can get. I love him for his imperfect Perfection!

CHAPTER 3

MY (S)HERO

Of course, I can't talk about my Daddy without talking about my mommy. My Mommy. I love my mommy so much. Like my Daddy, she has been there for me every step of the way. I don't have a childhood or adulthood memory that does not include my mommy. She has always been there for every milestone of my life. My mother had me at the age of eighteen. Being a young parent, she dropped out of high school in the twelfth grade. My mom went back and got her GED. She then went on to nursing school. I watched her accomplish her goal of becoming a Licensed Practical Nurse. I can remember the day of her graduation. My mom had on her white nursing dress and hat. She was so proud, and I was proud that she was my mommy. The family celebrated her graduation with dinner at her favorite restaurant. My Mommy. My (S)hero.

My mom made sure I had everything I needed throughout my childhood and mostly what I wanted. Because my dad was caught up in his addiction, my mom was often the primary provider. When my dad would "blow" his money on drugs, my mom made sure the bills were paid. My mom made sure we always had a roof over our heads and food on the table. She made sure our family never went without the things we needed. My Mommy. My (S)hero. She is such a strong woman.

You wouldn't recognize my mom's strength because she is so quiet. My mom has always been very calm and meek. Even in her meekness, my mom displayed a strength that I envy. It takes a different kind of strength to go through life with a drug-addicted husband. She went through so much dealing with the effects of my Daddy's addiction. As a protective mother often does, she attempted to hide those things from my sister and me. But addiction is something that can't be hidden. I can remember many times seeing and or hearing my mom crying over my dad's actions. Yet, my mother stayed in the fight. For us. My mom would say she stayed for my sister and me. She knew how much we loved our Daddy, and she did not want us to be without our Daddy. Truthfully, I don't think I could have personally stayed through the situations that my dad put my mom through. Strength. That takes a different type of strength. My Mommy. My (S)hero.

Because one of the traits of an addict is stealing, my mom would have to hide her personal belongings from my dad. She hid her purse. She hid her wallet separate from her purse. She hid her checkbook. She even hid her car keys. I can remember strangers knocking on our door to tell my mom that my dad owed them money. My mom would pay it if she had it. She paid off his drug debts. I can remember times when she would have to pay the drug dealer to get her car back. My dad would leave the house in my mom's car and not come back. She would search for him and find her car parked in dark areas. She would pay the dealer to retrieve the keys to her car. Dealing with these types of incidents is not for the weak. Mom was not weak. Strength was and still is her alter ego name. My Mommy. My (S)hero.

When I became pregnant, although she didn't verbalize her feelings, I knew my mom was supportive of me and the pregnancy. She went with me to every single doctor's appointment. She was there when we found out the sex of the baby. She was there during my morning sickness. She was there during the delivery. My mom helped me when I came home with Joel, my newborn baby. She was there in the wee hours of the night for feedings and crying spells. My mom helped me to learn motherhood. She was a great example! Joel was, and still is, the apple of her eye. Her first grandchild. Her first grandson. From the time he entered this world, my mom has made herself present and supportive of him. You would think that I spoiled Joel. Not even close to the spoiling that my mom continues to give him. My mom became one of Joel's primary caretakers.

The semester after I had Joel, I returned to school full-time and worked part-time. I couldn't have done it without my

(S)hero. When Joel started daycare, I dropped him off in the mornings and headed to my classes on campus. My mom would pick him up in the afternoon so that I could go to work. Because I worked until closing, she also made him dinner, bathed him, and put him to bed. Between my mom and his paternal grandmother, Joel was cared for and well-loved. This was his routine until he started school. During Joel's life, my mom has not missed a single milestone. She was there for his first smile, first crawl, first step, and first words. Just like my Daddy, mom was present for every game that my son played in sports. From age four until his high school graduation, my mother was at every game and track meet.

My mom was there for Joel's preschool graduation, elementary graduation, middle school graduation, and high school graduation. She was there for his college days, his first apartment, and his first baby–he only has one–Thank God! My Mom. My (S)hero. Just as she did for Joel, she has not missed a step with her first great-grandchild, her first great-granddaughter, Jaidynn. She is just as much a granny to Jaidynn as she has always been to Joel. Even as an adult, my mom continues to "granny" Joel. My Mommy. My (S)hero.

My mom has been by my side my entire life. She supported me through elementary, middle, and high schools. She supported me through college. She was present at every graduation. My mom was there when I got married. She helped me plan my wedding and make decisions. My mom accepted my husband and stepchildren with open arms. Matt, my bonus son that I raised, quickly became her second grandson. She did not miss a beat with him. Like Joel, she was there for his middle school graduation, high school graduation, all of his sports activities, and the birth of his first child, Kendall—my mom's second great-grandchild. Her second great-granddaughter. My mom loves her the ways she loves Matt. My mom was there throughout my marriage and my divorce. My mom has always been there for me. My Mommy. My (S)hero.

Let me tell you a little more about my (S)hero. My mom is not very sociable. She is a quiet woman of very few words. She has never been a smoker or drinker. My mom is very fashionable. I can remember her always making sure she was cute and kept her hair done. She loves her figure and is not afraid to show it off by dressing in clothes to accent her curves. My mom always says, "Your butt and hips are what make your figure!" She loves to dress up and never wears activewear or tennis shoes. My mom is a Christian woman. She is a Saved woman and Evangelist. However, she no longer preaches due to circumstances beyond her control. God has Blessed and watched over my mommy. Lord, I thank You for your protecting powers!

My mom is a nurse by profession. However, she is no longer working due to a disability. In 1997, my mom, sister, and little cousin were in a serious car accident. My mom's car was hit by an eighteen-wheel truck. It was a hit and run. While my sister and cousin had mild injuries and were taken to a hospital in Virginia, my mother was airlifted to a hospital in Tennessee due to her head injury. She suffered a severe head injury, requiring two surgeries. My mom spent several weeks in the hospital in Tennessee. Once she was stable enough for transport, she was transported by ambulance to the hospital back home in Lexington. My mom spent one week in a rehabilitation facility before she was discharged home. My mom's progress was nothing short of a miracle! A Blessing! Doctors said she would have to learn how to walk again, talk again, eat, and care for herself. But God! My mommy pulled through and was back living on her own in a short time. My Mommy. My (S)hero.

CHAPTER 4

IT'S REAL LOVE

Now that I have told you about my parents individually, let me tell you about them as a couple. My parents have a unique love story. They met at a young age and fell in love. My mom was fourteen, and my dad was eighteen. After dating off and on for four years, my mom became pregnant with me when she was eighteen years old. They got married when I was five years old and stayed married for eighteen years. My parents divorced in 1998. Their marriage was not always full of tears and pain. There were plenty of happy times. My dad would make my mom smile all the time. My dad would smile every time he looked at my mom. I remember the smiles, looks of admiration, words of affirmations, and love taps passed between my parents. I can remember them slow dancing in the living room.

My dad would sing love songs to my mom. Yes, my Daddy can sing! Over the years, he was in several singing groups. From R&B to Gospel, my Daddy can sing! One of my favorite memories is watching my dad and his friends practice singing.

The group was called the Climatics. My favorite song to hear them sing was "Float On" by The Floaters. The same admiration and smile I wore was reflected on my mom's face as she watched my Daddy. My parents loved one another. They would dress up in the same colors and go on dates. They would leave the house in a loving vibe and return even more in love. We had plenty of family time when we would just spend time watching movies and eating popcorn. They would cuddle up on the couch with one another. My parents loved each other so much. They still do!

My parents have a special relationship. They still talk regularly and spend time together. Over the years, they have taken vacations together, just the two of them. They take the grandkids on vacation together. They will randomly go on dates to the movies or out to eat. Just recently, my sister and I showed up at the movie theater where we knew our parents would be–one of their many dates together. They had been to brunch and then went to the movies. Yes, my sister and I busted up their date. New Year's Day 2021 was spent at the movies with our nuclear family– My Mommy. My Daddy. My Sissy. I love my family!

As you can see, my parents have a genuine love and friendship with each other. I love my parents' relationship, although they are no longer married. Our family is so close-knit that we do ALL things together. We take vacations together and celebrate all things together–holidays, birthdays, and "just because days." It's always my mom, my dad, my sister's family, and my family.

If you did not know my family personally, you would think my parents were still married. When you see them together, you can see the love they share–the love they have always shared. To this date, neither of my parents have remarried. They have both expressed a desire to remarry, but I often wonder how things would change if either of them were to remarry. I love my mommy and Daddy. I want them both to be happy. I want their hearts' desires to be fulfilled. I have to accept whatever God's plan is for them. Together or not–I love my parents. My Daddy. I am a Daddy's Girl. My Mommy. My (S)hero.

PART II
THE FACE

CHAPTER 5

SEXUAL ABUSE OR CHILD'S PLAY

"I was molested by my uncle," I said very nonchalantly. This disclosure came out unexpectedly. We were sitting at a high-top table at a sports bar. The music was so loud that it was hard to talk over the songs. After I said those words, I felt numb. I could not believe I had just shared those words. As soon as the words left my mouth, I wanted to get up from my seat and run out of the bar.

My sister looked up at me as tears immediately sprung in her eyes. "What do you mean you were molested by our uncle? Who Leisha? When? Do mom and dad know?" Once the initial shock wore off, my sister began to cry. She let the tears flow down her face. I felt bad that she was crying. My intent was not to make my sister cry. It was not to ruin the evening. We were out to listen to some music, have a few drinks, and have a good time.

As I looked away from her, I wanted to get up and walk away from the table. Had I really disclosed this secret fact about my life, about our life? Why did it come out at this moment? Maybe it was the alcohol speaking. Perhaps I was feeling empowered at that moment. Whatever the reason, it was something I was no longer going to let stay dormant. I proceeded to tell my sister about "our" uncle who molested me when I was young, around five years old.

As child victims tend to do, I had buried that trauma deep down in a place where I could not remember it. For many, many years, I did not remember the abuse I had experienced at the hands of my uncle. It was not until my adulthood that I started to have flashbacks about those painful, traumatic situations with my uncle. I cannot remember my exact age, but I remember the timeframe. We were living in a house on Coral Street. According to my mom, we moved into the house when I was four. We were there for three years before we had to move out of that house due to foreclosure. This is the period when my mom first became aware of my dad's drug activities.

What I can remember is being alone with my uncle. Although he was not an adult, he was nine years older than me, one a teenager. I can remember him putting me in the tub and watching me wash up. When I got out, he laid me on my stomach as he proceeded to dry me off with a towel. I can remember feeling his hands rub against my butt; a few times, that is all it was. He would watch me wash up, and he would dry me off. His hands would linger and rub against my naked skin. Then he would stop and help me get dressed. Then, we would play. Although the rubbing was inappropriate, it may sound innocent enough to some people–just exploration between kids. However, I was not exploring; he was.

One day taking a bath turned into something "not so innocent." That day, my uncle put me in the tub. He did not stay while I washed up. He just told me to let him know when I was ready to get out. Once I washed up, I yelled to let him know that I was out of the tub. He came into the bathroom and wrapped my tiny body in a towel. He carried me to my bedroom. I liked when he picked me up and carried me around. We used to play a game where he would have to find me. If he found me, he would pick me up and take me to my bedroom. He would pretend he was going to drop me hard, but he would not hurt me.

This particular day, my uncle put me down on my stomach and proceeded to dry me off, as usual. Then something else happened. He was straddling me so that I could not move my legs. His body was heavy against mine. I heard him unbuckle his belt. Because of the subtle touches and rubs in the past, I knew that hearing him undoing his belt was going to be bad. I remember laying on my stomach thinking, *"Just let me up, uncle, please."* The next thing I felt was his 'penis' rubbing against my skin, on my butt, on my thighs. I can remember the feeling of wetness on my butt and between my legs. At that time, I did not know why his 'penis' was wet. I can remember his 'penis' touching and rubbing between my inner thighs and moving towards my "private part." As I laid there, I don't recall saying anything out loud to him. However, I was thinking to myself, "*Why is his 'thing' touching me? Why is it wet? Why is my butt wet? What is my uncle doing back there? I want my mommy! I want my Daddy! Please stop! Do not hurt me! Let's just go play outside.*" I just wanted it to stop. I recall this happening only one time at this age.

You are probably asking if I told anyone. Honestly, I don't remember saying a word about my uncle to anyone. My mom says that I told her about it. However, I do not remember the exact details of our conversation. Recently, I asked my mother if she remembered the incident. She said, "I remember you coming to me while I was asleep. I used to work the third shift, and I was sleeping at the time. You kept coming into the room, saying you had to tell me something. You said that your uncle made you pull down your pants. You did not say anything more to me about it." My mom paused and continued, "I told your dad, and we had a conversation with your aunt. I confronted your uncle and told him I would kill him if he ever touched you again. You were never left alone with him again."

As I listened to my mother explain the story to me, I could not remember any of that conversation. However, I did let her know that I was around my uncle several times after that incident. My uncle has always been in my life and my personal space. After the conversation, I guess it became a "family secret" because I don't recall any other discussions about it. *Family Secrets.* I wonder if any of my little cousins have that same "family secret" about my uncle. How many families have secrets?

Because my extended family is very close-knit, I was always around my uncle. As we got older, I would spend a lot of time at my grandmother's house—the same house where my uncle lived. We were close. I enjoyed being around my uncle. He was funny. He was cool. He was hip. It felt like we were closer in age. However, he was nine years older than I was. As a pre-teen, I can remember playing a game that we called Mommy and Daddy. I was always the mom. My uncle was always the dad. My cousin was always the child. My uncle and I would pretend to be married and have one child. We would talk to each other as if we were married adults, mimicking what we had seen and heard married adults do. During our pretend play, when it was nighttime, we would climb into the bed together. My uncle would "spoon" with me. I can remember feeling the heat of his breath on my neck. I can remember feeling the erection of his penis against my butt. He would take my hand and put it on his penis so I could feel his erection. I can remember hearing him moaning when my inexperienced hand would touch him. I was between the ages of twelve and fourteen. He was somewhere between the ages of twenty-one and twenty-three. This time, he was the adult. I was the child. This "play" went on for a few years. I never thought any more about it. Like before, I do not recall saying anything about this incident to an adult.

To this date, I have not had a meaningful conversation with my parents about the depths of what happened to me. Although I am putting the details on paper for the world to read, I am still not ready to talk about it. Self-Work. Healing.

It was not until my adulthood that I started to remember. I was at my best friend's house. We were eating, laughing, and enjoying "girl time." I had not seen her for a few years because she had moved away to another state. I was visiting with her. At some point, the conversation switched to a more serious discussion of family. It was during this time that she disclosed her uncle had molested her when she was a young girl.

Those four words jumped out at me. Uncle. Molested. Young. Girl. I suddenly felt as if I could not breathe. My airway felt tight. It was as if I was being suffocated by her words. The more she talked, the worse I felt. My throat became itchy and parched. I began to break out in a sweat. *Why am I sweating like this? What is going on?* I could not understand the physical reaction that I was having to her words. Uncle. Molested. Young. Girl. Why did those words haunt me at that moment? I became sick to my stomach and had to go lie down. I thought it was the snacks and wine coolers. Little did I know that I was having a physical reaction to my forgotten trauma. I had repressed those memories. For many, many years, I never thought or talked about it, but her words seemed to awaken memories deep inside me.

A few days later, I started to remember those shameful incidents. I could vividly see images of my uncle as a teenager. I began to remember the days of him drying me off after I had taken a bath. The thoughts and images kept coming until they took over my every thought. For several days, my mind was consumed with thoughts and images of my uncle. I could feel the bed beneath my young body. I could hear the unbuckling of his belt. I could feel the wetness of his penis against my butt. I felt like I was going crazy! *Why am I remembering this? Did this really happen? Am I making this up?* Repressed Memories.

Even as my mind started to replay the events on a nightly basis, the one emotion that I never felt was anger. I was never angry with my uncle. I was never afraid of my uncle. I love him. He is cool. He is funny. He is my uncle. It really confused me that I felt no anger towards my uncle, and because I have never displayed anger at my uncle, I started to question myself. Did I want that experience with him? Definitely not– not when I was a young child nor as a teenager. I felt guilty that I did not, and still do not, have any anger or resentment towards my uncle. I will never allow him to be alone with any child or grandchild of mine. Nevertheless, I do not have a problem being around him. He does not make me feel uncomfortable or scared. On the contrary, I care about him. He is my uncle. It is almost as if I am immune to having any emotions as it relates to him. Because of this, it makes me question, *"Was it simply Child's Play or Inappropriate Sexual Contact?"* It definitely was inappropriate sexual contact and child sexual abuse.

The impact on me became traumatic in my adulthood. I now understand those experiences caused me to have issues with love and trust, because I do not remember any real consequences for my uncle. I felt like there was no adult who believed and protected me. The fact is that it was "addressed," yet, for my entire life, my uncle has been at every family function. This says to me that no one took the allegations seriously. Maybe that is just it. They were allegations. Oftentimes in families, an accusatory statement is disclosed by a child, and no one believes them. The statement then becomes an "allegation." However, I am not mad at my family. As an adult, I made the decision to be around him. I invited him to my wedding, and he came. I do not regret those decisions because he is my uncle. But because I do not have underlying anger at my uncle, I feel ashamed. I question if there is something wrong with me for not feeling angry? I do not know. This past trauma and my emotions surrounding my memories will continue to be addressed in my self-work and counseling.

CHAPTER 6

MY GREATEST BLESSING

The Pregnancy: December 1993

"Boy, I am not pregnant. I don't know why you keep trying to put that on me." I looked at the little white stick that I had just peed on. In my mind, I knew I was not pregnant, but I was nervous, nonetheless. I patiently waited on the clear screen to show the negative symbol indicating I was not pregnant. "I'll call you back," I said into the phone as I hung it up. As I continued to wait for the results, I began to pray, *"God, please don't let me be pregnant. Please don't let me be pregnant."* I walked out of the bathroom and went to the front door. I wanted to make sure my mom did not come in the door before I could discard the pregnancy test in the outside garbage disposal.

Instead of the three minutes the directions said to wait, I waited five minutes. I walked back into the bathroom and picked up the small white stick. I looked at the stick, feeling confident that it was going to be negative. Tears immediately stung my eyes.

I could feel my blood pressure rise. The beating of my heart felt like it was going to burst through my chest. My mouth became dry. I could not say anything. "Noooooooooooo!" I was finally able to scream out as the realization that the negative sign (-) was actually a positive symbol (+) on the clear small screen. I took my right foot and kicked the wall. My size eight foot made an indention in the wall that looked like it was hit with a bowling ball. I fell to the floor and begin to cry. *"How did I get pregnant? How did I let this happen? This cannot be true. Pregnant, really?"* All types of thoughts were going through my head. *"If God was going to do this to me, why not let me be pregnant by my boyfriend? How will I explain to my boyfriend that I am pregnant by the person he caught me cheating with? What will my parents say? How will I explain this to them? How will I explain this to all my friends and family?"*

I had just spent good, quality time with my family just a few weeks ago on Thanksgiving. It is now December, and I just found out that I am pregnant. My estimated due date confirmed I had conceived in November, the first time I was with Joel's dad, and we were drinking Mad Dog (MD) 2020 wine. *How ironic is that?* I was under the influence of Mad Dog 2020 when I conceived Joel. The year 2020 is when Evolve: From Heart Breaks to Hearts Healed, my first published book, and subsequently, this book was conceived and birthed. The year 2020 is also when my self-work and healing began.

About a week later, I finally told my mom that I was pregnant. I confessed to her that I was pregnant by Joel's dad and not my current boyfriend. My mother was always quiet and reserved. She responded to my news by simply saying nothing. She looked at me and said, "Okay." I didn't know if that meant she was angry, disappointed, happy, or somewhere in-between. Maybe she didn't know what to say. My mother's lack of communication over something as major as a baby really confused me. Sometime over the next few days, my mom did tell my dad about the pregnancy. My dad, unlike my mom, came into my room and had a conversation with me about the pregnancy. He sat down on the bed next to me. I was nervous. I knew what he was coming to talk to me about, but I did not know what he was going to say. It was my first semester of college at the University of Kentucky. What is my dad going to say to me? Is he disappointed? Will he be angry? Will he be hurt? So many emotions went through my mind as I waited for him to speak.

"How do you feel?" He looked concerned as he questioned me. He put his arm around me and continued, "Whatever you're feeling or not feeling is okay. Pat and I are here for you, and we support you." As my dad assured me of his support, I allowed all the fear and anxiety to melt away. My dad always has a way of making me feel okay. Just as my dad promised, he and my mom were there with me, supporting me through every step of my pregnancy.

The Birth: August 11, 1994

This is the day that my life completely changed. My greatest blessing breathed his first breath at 10:33 a.m. I never thought I could love someone as much as I loved him. Joel DeShawn Brown Jr. I had just pushed him out after fifteen-and-one-half hours of labor. As I lay back on the cold, hard nursing bed waiting to hold my son for the first time, I looked at my mother. She had a look of concern on her face. Something is wrong. I looked at my son's father. He had the biggest smile on his face. He looked like he just witnessed a miracle. Well, he did witness a miracle. Childbirth is a miracle in itself. Have you ever witnessed the birth of a child? I have witnessed it twice. It is the most amazing experience I could ever have. No one should ever question if God is real after witnessing the birth of a human being. Five fingers. Five toes. Breathing.

The look of concern was confirmed when the doctor took my son out of the room before I could even touch him. My mother's face continued to look nervous. Immediately, I knew there was something wrong. I asked everyone, "What's going on? Why can't I see my son?" I was told my son was having trouble breathing and that he had jaundice. He had to be assisted with breathing and put under light immediately. I did not see my son until six hours later. It was 4:20 p.m. when I finally held my son for the first time. *He was perfect. His odd-shaped head was perfect. His smile was perfect. Five perfect fingers on each hand. Five perfect toes on each foot. My son was perfect.*

As I held my son, admiring his sweet face, I thought back over the last twenty-four hours. I had a doctor's appointment on August 9th. The doctor examined me and told me I had another four weeks to go. Then, he sent me for an ultrasound.

"He's really small," the doctor told me. "I'm concerned about his size. I would like to see him gain another pound before he makes his entrance." His words concerned me, but I was young. In my mind, my son would be fine, no need to worry. As I left the doctor's office with my mom, I called Joel's dad to update him about our son. He sounded so excited as he spoke about his junior. Yes, Junior. He literally yelled out loud, with the biggest smile on his face, and called his mom as soon as the nurse told us to get ready for our baby boy.

Although I wanted a baby girl, I could not keep my excitement about having a son under control. I immediately started buying baby clothes for my son. After shopping in a few stores, my mom and I finally made it home. As we were walking into the house, I could hear the phone ringing. I ran and picked it up, "Hello."

"Can I speak to Deleisha Webb, please?" After letting the caller know that this was Deleisha, the caller continued. *"This is Dr. O'Neil. After reviewing your ultrasound pictures and consulting with a few of my colleagues, we decided it's best to*

induce your labor. The baby is fully developed and cannot wait another four weeks. Can you report to the hospital tomorrow at 4:00 p.m.?" Let me share an interesting fact—the same doctor who delivered my son was the same doctor who delivered me, Dr. O'Neil, at Central Baptist Hospital. I will never forget him.

As I hung up the phone, I started to cry and yelled for my mom. She came running from her bedroom asking what is wrong. I told her that the doctor wants me to report to the hospital tomorrow at 4:00 p.m. for an induction. After calling my dad to inform him as well, I called MD to let him know that I would be at the hospital tomorrow afternoon.

On Wednesday, August 10, my mom, dad, and I arrived at Central Baptist Hospital at 4:00 p.m. Joel's dad and his family met us there as well. By 6:00 p.m., I was settled in my labor, delivery, and recovery room, with an IV injected into my right arm. By 8:00 p.m., the contractions were starting. I suffered those painful contractions for eight hours before I asked, no begged, for an epidural. By 10:00 a.m. Thursday morning, I had finally dilated ten centimeters. Although I was ready to meet my son, I became nervous as the staff got the room ready for birthing. Before I could start pushing, my son's heart rate dropped, and I was transferred to a delivery room. The delivery room resembled a surgical room with all of the high-tech equipment. Because of the quick transfer, I immediately thought something was wrong with my son.

It was a successful delivery. I looked down at my baby boy and lifted him to my nose to smell his baby breath. He looked so peaceful. So relaxed. So calm. So beautiful. I would not trade those fifteen and one-half hours of labor for anything. My baby boy was six pounds nine ounces and eighteen and one-half inches long. My son was born healthy, and I was a proud mother.

After my son was born, he became my primary focus for living. To make sure I gave my son the best life possible, I finished college so I could get a good-paying job. I continued my education and received a graduate degree. Although I wanted these things for myself, it was more important for me to have the degrees to be able to get a job that paid me a decent wage. I quickly learned how expensive it was to raise a child. It began with childcare. The cost of childcare alone cut my paychecks in half. I was able to receive childcare assistance to help offset some of those fees. I was *blessed* to have the support of my mom and Joel's paternal family to help with raising Joel.

Joel started playing sports at the age of four. His love for sports continued until he graduated from high school. Joel played T-ball, baseball, football, basketball, and ran track. He played sports for Parks & Rec Centers and privately owned Amateur Athletic Union (AAU) Travel Baseball and Basketball teams. Once in middle school, he played football in the fall, basketball in the winter, and ran track in the spring. All while continuing to play AAU Travel Basketball. The sports life continued in high school. Joel was passionate about his sports. As his mother, I was passionate about making sure he had everything he needed when it came to his participation in sports. I made sure that Joel was able to play on the AAU Traveling teams as well. My life became a sports mom. No complaints though, it was my honor to support my son. He was a great kid academically. Joel was an A student in elementary and made A/B Honor Roll every year in middle and high schools. He was a polite and respectful kid.

For many, many, many years, I continued to make him my priority. So much so that I didn't allow him to do things on his own. Those teenage years when it's important for boys to be taught the skills and tools of manhood, my son missed those moments. As his mother, I did not allow anyone to have access to my son. Not even my now ex-husband. My dad was the only man that I allowed to have any "real" connection with Joel. I've already told you about my Daddy. Although his influence was positive, it wasn't the fatherly influence that he needed. Joel's dad wasn't ever active in Joel's life. Yes, he was there, but he wasn't actively involved. It was me. His mother. A woman. Because Joel was my baby, I coddled Joel. I did everything for him. I didn't allow Joel to learn how to stand on his own. At the time, I didn't realize that I was doing him a disservice.

As Joel got older (late teens), I started to see a change in him. He began to exhibit explosive behaviors when he couldn't get his way or get what he wanted. He would have episodes of lashing out in anger. When I think back over his childhood years, I can recall two other times when he had an explosive outbreak. Because he was so young, he was unable to verbal his anger. I spent many nights having serious talks with him about why he was angry. He never could identify a reason. I can guess that it was related to not having his father around. I can guess that it was related to my dad's drug addiction. I can guess it was related to me being a young mother. I can make many guesses. However, the anger was never identified.

I think Joel buried his anger for a while, but then it started to show itself again in his late teens. I bet you can guess how I responded. You guessed it right. I made excuses for him. I placed blame on myself as a mother–codependency and enabling. Just as I did with my dad, I took ownership of Joel's issues instead of making him responsible for his own behaviors and outbursts. Don't get me wrong; I believe the lack of parental involvement played a huge role in my son's life. Most of his friends' dads were around and active in their life. Joel's was not. For that, I blamed myself and carried the guilt.

Joel graduated from high school with honors and went to college. He attended St. Augustine College for two semesters and then transferred to Lenoir-Rhyne University. He took up accounting but did not finish his degree. Although a young adult, Joel was still my baby. I continued to do things for him that he should have been doing for himself. A disservice. Degree or no degree, I am so proud of my son for graduating from high school with honors and going to college. Joel became a father on his nineteenth birthday. Joel and Jaidynn share the same birthday. A day I will never forget. Joel cried through the entire labor and delivery. He's such an emotional guy. During the actual delivery, he cried so much that the nurses were making sure he was okay and that nothing was wrong with him. While he was holding Jaidynn, doing skin-to-skin, the nurses came in and sang Happy Birthday to both him and Jaidynn. It was the sweetest gesture. He continued to cry. Talk about a Proud Mommy and Proud Nana that day–August 11, 2015.

Several months later, Joel got a full-time job at Wells Fargo. He bought a brand-new car and moved out on his own. Proud Mommy. Fast forward to today. My son is twenty-six years old and finally learning to be his own man. That development was slow because I had enabled him most of his life. A disservice. It wasn't until his adulthood that I realized how much damage I had done to my son by not allowing him to be a man. To stand on his own two feet. To make decisions and live with those consequences. I was so busy "protecting" him from life that life got the best of him.

Joel went through a dark period where he was making bad decisions and not owning his actions. He blamed everyone else for his bad decisions. He blamed me for not allowing him to live life on his own terms. Can you see the Codependency and Enabling?

See how it flowed over from my dad to my son? For a long time, I took ownership of Joel's "stuff." His bad decisions. His negative attitude. His anger. His explosiveness. His lack of positive parenting. I felt as if I was responsible for all of his "stuff" because I am his mother. The same way I have always done with my dad. It wasn't until this summer, during the Pandemic, that I learned to release all those things.

I am learning a different, healthier way of being there for Joel as an adult. Parenting a child is different from being a parent to an adult child. Parenting is one of my life's greatest blessings. Parenting has also been one of my hardest struggles. There is no rulebook on parenting. You learn as you grow. As an adult, my son and I have had some *challenging* days, months, and years. We have had the "*I love you more than anything in this world*" days. We have had some "*I have to love you from a distance*" days. Several months ago, we had more of the *"I have to love you from a distance type of days."*

It has been so bad that we decided to participate in family counseling. Yes, counseling. Family counseling was the best move we could have made. We learned so much about each other. I thought I knew all about my son. Wrong. Because we were both vulnerable and open to the process, we were able to be completely honest and talk about the hard things. I gained a new respect for him as my adult son. He gained a new respect for me as his mother. I saw changes in Joel that I knew weren't anything but his determination and God. Family counseling turned into individual counseling for him; I was already in individual counseling. The insight he gained in counseling began to show in positive ways. Joel began to journal. His attitude changed. His talk changed. His walk changed. His outlook on life changed. His parenting changed. Proud Mommy. Despite it all, parenting is still my life's greatest blessing!

This letter, from my son, displays his adult journey:

Dear Mom

I cannot thank you enough for the sacrifices you have made for me throughout my life. You have taken every precaution to make sure that I become the best black man I can be. I know that the path was not easy, but you accomplished your goal. You raised a black child to become a black man in America, destroying the statistics. Your child has a clean criminal record and has never been behind bars. Most importantly, I am still living and able to make a presence in this world today. I am not denying the mishaps throughout my years, but when I ventured off, you steered me back on the right path. I am now taking in your skills and trying to replicate them for my amazing daughter and future kids to come.

This brings me to the point, the most significant thing that has ever happened in my life, period; the birth of my first-born child, "Jaidynn Rose Marie Brown." There was nothing simple about the process;, me still being a young man trying to figure out my path in life, I thought I was not ready. When I first found out Jai's mother was pregnant, I battled internally with my emotions. I knew I wasn't in the spot in life I wanted to be when having my first child, but all that went out the window, I had to prepare myself mentally; there was no other option. I regret not being more attentive to Jai's mother while she carried my child; I was young and not making smart decisions. I was being irresponsible and got another girl pregnant, though she ended up aborting the baby. At the time, I was ignorant of the real meaning of having a child. After talks with you and my aunt, I had to have a sit down with myself and reevaluate what was important to me. In that moment, I realized I was no longer just living for myself; every decision I make from now until I die will affect my child's life. I decided to love her with every drop of blood in my body, and on her birth date, I felt every bit of that love.

The morning of 08/11/2015, I woke up feeling like heaven and earth collided. One reason being because I had reached what society has deemed the "dream age" 21. For years and years, kids and teens make extravagant plans for the time when they turn 21. I always thought I would do the typical 21st birthday celebration where I would go out, party, drink, etc. However, this was no typical birthday. I woke up that morning in the hospital waiting on my newborn to arrive. When she was born, I knew I had received the greatest birthday gift a man could possibly receive, my firstborn child born on my 21st birthday. Therefore, instead of the norm, I had a birthday celebration unique than most, started my day by cutting the umbilical cord while the new grandmothers in the room recording the birth. Usually, I try not to let people see me cry, but the streams couldn't stop flowing from my eyes. Tears of joy, of course, while also thinking of all the different ways I am going to protect and serve my baby. Because it was my 21st birthday, my ID expired that day, so afterward, I had to leave and go straight to the DMV for a new driver's license so that I could be able to sign the birth certificate. Mall trip and then back to the hospital to spend the rest of our birthday with my baby. Though it was not a typical birthday, it was the best birthday I have had. I am so grateful for Jaidynn and I try to show her how much I love her all the time. She takes notice of my TLC (Tender Loving Care) and reciprocates it. She is Daddy's little angel despite what anybody says or thinks, and I will protect her to the end, for she was the beginning of my adulthood.

Sincerely,

Your Son, A Black Man!

CHAPTER 7

THE GRANDPARENTS & SUPPORT CIRCLE

My Mom. My Dad. Joel's granny, Jewel. Joel's granddaddy, Charles. These important and supportive people were involved in my son's upbringing. Without their support, I don't know how I would have made it. As an infant, my mom and Granny Jewel cared for Joel while I worked and attended school full-time. Joel's paternal grandmother, Granny Jewel, lived in Louisville, Kentucky. Oftentimes, Joel would stay with her for three to four days at a time. During that time, I was able to work, attend classes, and get my schoolwork completed without any interruption. When Joel was with me, I was constantly on the go. I dropped him off at daycare in the morning. I went to class. After class, I went to work until the evening hours. My mother would pick him up from daycare. By the time I got off work and picked up Joel, he was asleep for the night. I felt so guilty. I felt like I was failing my son. This was our regular routine for the first four years of Joel's life. He was back and forth between Lexington and

Louisville. Grandparents. They have and continue to play such a vital role in my son's life.

Even as an adult, Joel will reminisce about things Granny Jewel said and did for him. Talk about spoiling a grandchild–Granny Jewel took Joel shopping to get everything he wanted every single time she had him. From toys to food to snacks. Joel was spoiled rotten by her. Granny Jewel passed away on August 12, 2012. The day after Joel's eighteenth birthday. It was the weekend he moved into his first college dorm. Granny Jewel was the first major loss in Joel's life, and it hurt him so badly. The blessing is that we had just seen her about a week before she passed away. She was sick in the hospital for a while. We made a surprise visit to Louisville and got to visit her in the hospital. She was completely shocked and happy to see him. I remember the last words they said to each other. Joel hugged and kissed Granny Jewel on the cheek. He asked her if she needs anything. Granny Jewel looked at him and said, "You pray for me, and I'll pray for you!" She smiled and thanked us for coming to see her. Still today, at the age of twenty-six, Granny Jewel continues to make an impact in Joel's life. Joel thinks of her often and just smiles. #RIH Granny Jewel. We love you.

Granny and Granddaddy. My mom and dad have always been and continue to be a huge support for Joel. He and my dad have a strong relationship. My dad is his confidant, his voice of reason, and his pain in the butt at times. My dad has always attempted to steer Joel on the straight path towards adulthood. My mom is a true "Granny" to Joel. As a child, she would be there for his every need. He could call her for *anything,* and she would come running. She also supported his every sport–basketball, baseball, football, track–she was there. My mom was there for every major milestone. Elementary graduation. Middle school graduation. High school graduation. College move-in weekend. My mom never misses a beat. She is also his #1 fan, and she lets him know this on a regular basis. Even today, although it is unhealthy enabling, my mom will do Joel's laundry. Pick up his clothes. Wash his clothes. Fold his clothes and drop them back off to him. But she also encourages him, loves on him, and gives him advice. Grandparents. I can't imagine the outcome of my son's life without their influence. They are wise, they are essential, they are fun, and they are connected.

According to Altura Learning, Grandparents are key to grandchildren's development. Here is why Altura Learning says Grandparents are key to children's development:

Grandparents are wise. "A lifetime of experiences has shaped a grandparent into who he or she is. Because grandparents have weathered the ups and downs of life, they make excellent advice-givers and problem-solvers, storing a wealth of practical knowledge."

Grandparents are essential. "The love that grandparents feel for their grandchildren is especially strong, amplified by the love they bear for their own children. Grandparents are the part of the formation and maintenance of the traditions that define family. They possess memories that later generations can understand only through stories, and insights into culture and heritage that serve as a legacy for children and grandchildren alike."

Grandparents are fun. "Grandparents can offer a relaxed perspective and remind a family to remain light-hearted. It is highly beneficial for families to set aside time for having fun, and even upon becoming adults, many grandchildren look back fondly on the childhood memories they have playing games with their grandparents."

Grandparents are connected. "By offering love and guidance, imparting wisdom, passing on traditions, and making memories, grandparents can leave behind a legacy that their grandchildren will value for the rest of their lives."

Not only are my parents EXCELLENT grandparents, they are also EXCELLENT great-grandparents. I have a five-year-old granddaughter. Joel's daughter, Jaidynn, was born on his 21st birthday. My parents were right there. Again, as great-grandparents, they have not missed a single milestone in Jaidynn's short life. The exact same gentleness, love, care, and support that they've always provided to Joel, has been extended to Jaidynn. They love Jaidynn and Jaidynn loves her granny Pat and granddaddy. This same level of love and support applies to my other grandbaby, my bonus son's daughter, Kendall. My parents are there for her as well. My parents are the true definition of grandparents, and I appreciate them more than they will ever know!

It wasn't just the grandparents who were key in Joel's younger years. Joel's paternal great-grandmother, Granny Della, and his great-aunt, Aunt Joyce, were also key during his younger life and supportive of him. As Joel got older and didn't want to spend as much time in Louisville, he would spend a lot of time with Aunt Joyce, Granny Jewel's sister, and Granny Della, Granny Jewel's mother. They have always been supportive of Joel and me. They provided emotional, physical, and financial support in his dad's absence. Even after his dad was released from prison, the paternal family continued to be actively engaged in Joel's life. Still today, I could go to the family if we needed anything, and if they have it, we have it! The Brown family has made a huge impact in both of our lives. I'm appreciative of all of those in my circle of support! My mom! My dad! My sister! Granny Jewel! Granny Della! Aunt Joyce! I have to acknowledge my extended family as well. I THANK YOU ALL!

CHAPTER 8

THE CALLING

The Fayette County Court–Family Court. My very first professional job. I was a clerk for the Judges in Family Court. This position is where I discovered the "calling" that God had for my life. When God speaks to you, HE speaks to you. I quickly learned this lesson once I became a working adult.

Upon graduating from high school in 1993, I already knew what my educational plans were. I wanted to attend college for Computer Science. I wanted to be a Computer Programmer. In the fall of 1993, I enrolled full-time at the University of Kentucky. I never teetered about the decision to major in Computer Science. I always enjoyed working with numbers and computers. My favorite subject in school was always math. I declared my major Computer Science. I finished my first and second year with ease. School was always a breeze for me, even college courses. I never had to study. The information came naturally to me once I reviewed it. That is, until college Calculus. I took Calculus 1 and passed the class with a C. I had learned the main concepts of

Calculus 1 in Pre-Calculus during my senior year of high school. Calculus 2 was hard, but I managed to pass with a D average. However, that was not good enough to advance. A degree in Computer Science required Calculus 4. At the University of Kentucky, I could not move on to the next level of Calculus unless I passed the previous course with a C or better. I took Calculus 2 a second time. This time, I attended the math lab twice a week, and I had tutoring. I passed the class with a low C and was able to enroll in Calculus 3.

By this time, I was entering my third year of college. I decided to transfer to Lexington Community College to take Calculus 3. Because it was a community college, I felt like the class would be easier. I was wrong. I quickly learned that Calculus 3 is Calculus 3 no matter where I take the course. I struggled.

The description of Calculus 3 at the University of Kentucky is as follows:

> "The important concepts of Calculus 3, also called Multivariable Calculus, include vectors and geometry of space, three-dimensional vector calculus, partial derivatives, doubled and triple integrals, integration on surfaces, and Greens Theorem" (www.math.as.uky.edu).

Does any of this sound easy to you? Me either. I continued to struggle. I studied every single day for this course. I did not comprehend it. I was able to complete assignments because I could reference my notes and study guides. However, I did not do as well on tests and quizzes. I did not comprehend enough to move on to Calculus 4. I decided to meet with my college advisor to discuss my options. After reviewing my transcript, my advisor informed me that I had three options. 1) Apply for my Associate Degree in Business Management and be done with school. I only needed one more class for this degree. 2) Pass Calculus 3 with a grade of C or better and return to the University of Kentucky (UK) to advance on to Calculus 4, which I would have to pass to receive a bachelor's degree in Computer Science–no exceptions; or 3) Return to the UK, change my major and take Computer Science off the table. I was a single mother with a 2-year-old. I was working twenty to thirty hours a week while attending school full-time. I was tired, and I wanted to be done. Although my major was Computer Science, many of my electives were in human behavior and social welfare policy. After reviewing my transcript in detail, my advisor pointed out that I could get my bachelor's degree in one year if I switched my major to Family Studies. I made the decision to take the final course needed in Family Studies, and I graduated from Lexington Community College with an associate degree.

Three months later, I returned to the University of Kentucky and enrolled full-time to work on my bachelor's degree. After four semesters, I graduated in May 1999 with my Bachelor's Degree in Family Studies. After four-and-one-half years of full-time college schooling, I was done. So, I thought.

My first job after receiving my bachelor's degree was with the Fayette County Courthouse Family Court Division. My position title was full-time Clerk of Courts. One of the first cases that I clerked for was a court case involving a mother who taught her nine-year-old daughter how to perform oral sex using a goat. Yes. Goat. The family lived on a farm with many farm animals–pigs, cows, horses, chickens, and goats. The child came to the attention of Child Welfare because she was acting out sexually in school. The child was making sexually inappropriate comments to other students. She was making inappropriate sexual gestures such as sticking her hands down her pants and touching herself. She also attempted to put her hands down a classmate's pants.

After several incidents of inappropriate sexual behaviors and a phone call home to her mother, the school counselor made a report to the Child Abuse Hotline. After investigating the allegations, the nine-year-old Caucasian girl was removed from her mother's physical and legal custody. The child was placed in a treatment facility for sexually abused children. This case was horrible. The courts eventually terminated the mother's parental rights, and the child's goal was changed from "reunification" to "adoption." My heart ached for this little girl. Her life was full of pain and trauma at such a young age. Her adult uncle molested her when she was only four years old. Her older brother, who was six years older, was having sex with her when she was seven. In addition, her mother was teaching her how to perform oral sex on farm animals. It was also suspected that her mother was prostituting her out to older men. However, those allegations were never proven. By the time I left the agency, the child had not been adopted and had been placed from a treatment facility to foster homes back to treatment facilities. This position was my introduction to Child Welfare.

In October 2000, I began working for the Department of Social Services Family Services Division–Child Welfare. One of the saddest cases I worked on involved a single mother, her ten-year-old son, and her boyfriend. I was in my office working on documentation. With child welfare, there is always plenty of documentation to be completed. It was my "paperwork" day. The day I dedicated to staying in my office and being caught up on documentation and other paperwork. At this point, I had been doing child abuse investigations for about two years. Talk about having a passion for something; I had and still have a true passion for working in child welfare–protecting children and educating families. My boss called me into his office. "Dee, I need you to take this case for me. I know you're not supposed to be in rotation today, but it's a sexual abuse investigation, and I need you."

I looked at Gary. He was aging. His gray beard was growing wildly. He always had a "gruff" look, but today that look was intensified by the tiredness of his eyes. They were red and looked exhausted. "Sure, what is it?" I asked as I took the paper from his hand. I sat down in the metal chair on the opposite side of Gary's desk. I looked over the identifying information–child's age, race, mother's name, age, etc. I read the allegations silently. After reading it twice, I looked at Gary. "This sounds pretty bad, Gary."

"Yeah, that's why I want you to work the case. Can you go to the facility today?"

"Yes, I'll go ahead and shut down and head there now," I told Gary as I walked out of his office. Although it was my day to work in the office, I was okay leaving. It would feel good to get out of the building. Besides, working in the field is one of the things I loved about the job.

When I walked into the room, I sat at the round table with all of the staff who work with Isaiah. I took in the brightly decorated room. There were splashes of bright colors on every wall. Handprints of kids of all sizes in different colors covered the wall. Introductions were made once everyone who had been invited to the meeting had arrived. The participants included me, the child abuse investigator, Detective Gore and Detective Allen from the Fayette County Police Department, Crimes against Children, Ms. Johnson, Isaiah's mother, and three staff from the treatment facility.

Everyone in the room cringed as the details of Isaiah's sexual abuse were described by the therapist. This case was one of the saddest I had heard in my two years at the agency. The therapist restated the story as Isaiah had told it to her.

Ms. Johnson and her boyfriend had been together for five years. The boyfriend began to groom Isaiah a few years back. The behaviors that were described mimicked the stages of grooming. The professionals around the table recognized the signs as described by the therapist.

According to Elizabeth L. Jeglic Ph.D., *Psychology Today* (2019), there are six stages of grooming:

Victim selection. The first stage of sexual grooming often involves selecting a victim. Studies have found that victims are often selected due to their perceived physical <u>attractiveness</u>, ease of access, or perceived vulnerability. Children who may have less parental supervision are at particular risk. Further, child molesters may also target children who have low <u>self-esteem</u>, low <u>confidence</u>, or who may be unduly trusting or naïve (Jeglic, E.L. 2019).

In this case, Isaiah is an only child and had no father figure in his life. Isaiah also has developmental delays. He was ten years old but functioned on the level of a six-year-old. Ms. Johnson was low functioning, as well, and had borderline mild mental retardation (MMR). According to the American Psychiatric Association (DSM-5), mild mental retardation is now termed Intellectual Development Disorder (APA_DSM-5-Intellectual-Disability.pdf, 2013). Johnson's boyfriend may not have targeted the family, but once becoming involved with them, he realized Isaiah and his mother were easy targets.

Gaining access. During the second stage of the grooming process, the offender seeks to gain access to the child by separating them emotionally and physically from their guardians. In cases where the child molester is a family member, they have easier access to the child. In fact, in almost half of family abuse cases, the abuse takes place in the child's bedroom after everyone is asleep (Jeglic, E.L. (2019).

Both Ms. Johnson and Isaiah were trusting of her boyfriend. It was easy to separate Isaiah physically from Ms. Johnson. The boyfriend would spend a lot of time with Isaiah alone. They would go for walks to get food, candy, and play at the park. A great deal of Isaiah's abuse occurred outside of the home when he was alone with his mom's boyfriend. There was no need to separate Isaiah from his mom emotionally because of the low intellectual functioning.

When the abuser is not a family member, the access stage becomes more complicated. Thus, these predators often take positions in the community where they can be in contact with minors without suspicion, such as volunteer work or employment with children, or a charitable foundation. They may also befriend single parents and offer to pick up or care for the child to help the parent out (Jeglic, E.L. (2019).

There you have it. Ms. Johnson was a single parent and welcomed assistance in caring for Isaiah. Ms. Johnson's boyfriend would meet Isaiah at the bus stop and walk him home. He became the babysitter for Isaiah while Ms. Johnson was at work. Ms. Johnson was grateful to have help with Isaiah and not have to worry about his care while she was working.

Trust development. In the third stage of sexual grooming, the abuser works to gain the trust of the victim, their guardian(s) and the community so that they can engage in the abuse without detection. During this stage, the offender works to gain the trust of the intended victim by giving them small gifts, special <u>attention</u>, or sharing secrets. This makes the child feel special and gives them the belief that they have a caring relationship with the perpetrator.

These types of behaviors will change depending upon the age of the child. For younger children, it may involve playing games, going on outings, or getting presents, while for adolescents it may involve the discussion of their personal lives, access to <u>cigarettes</u>, drugs, or <u>alcohol</u>, and sharing "secrets" that they do not tell their guardians.

During this period, the perpetrator may also work to groom the guardian not to believe the child by telling the guardian that the child is acting out or telling lies (Jeglic, E.L. (2019).

Ms. Johnson's boyfriend would take Isaiah out for food, ice cream, or candy. On one occasion, he took Isaiah to get pizza. After pizza, they stopped at an ice cream parlor, and Isaiah was given two scoops of his favorite ice cream. On the way back home, they stopped at Walmart, and he bought Isaiah a basketball. On the weekends, Ms. Johnson's boyfriend would take the time to play basketball with Isaiah. Isaiah did not have many friends, so his mom's boyfriend became his friend. As the friendship grew, the trust grew as well. Ms. Johnson's boyfriend quickly gained the trust of Isaiah and his mother.

Desensitization to touch. This is generally the last stage of the grooming process before the actual abuse begins. During this stage of grooming, the abuser increases the non-sexual touching that will prepare the child for the abuse. For instance, this may include hugs, snuggles, wrestling, and tickling.

Other tactics include taking a bath/shower together, swimming in the nude, drying a child off with a towel, giving massages, or showing the child pornography.

At this stage, the perpetrator may also start discussing sexual behaviors and content with the child/adolescent so that they feel more comfortable with this type of material.

Ultimately, the goal of sexual grooming is to provide the perpetrator the opportunity to offend against the child without detection (Jeglic, E.L. (2019).

Isaiah had described a game that he and his mom's boyfriend would play. His mom's boyfriend would tickle him between his legs, and he could not laugh. The object of the game was to see how long Isaiah could be tickled between his legs before he laughed aloud. Isaiah reported that the longer he could be tickled without laughing, the better his prize was for the game. He used the example of getting candy before he ate dinner if he did not laugh for a long time. Isaiah also described playing "hide-n-seek" with his mom's boyfriend. He would hide, and his mom's boyfriend would have to find him. When he found him, Isaiah reported they would hug tight and say in unison, "Don't let me go."

Ms. Johnson reported observing her boyfriend tickling and hugging Isaiah on a regular basis. They would often watch a movie as a family, and Isaiah and her boyfriend would sit on the couch together while Ms. Johnson would sit in a chair alone. Ms. Johnson reported they would be "hugged up" on the couch. However, she never questioned the behaviors because she was appreciative Isaiah was receiving the male companionship he longed for. Ms. Johnson was grateful for the attention he was giving her son.

These sexual grooming techniques will confuse the child as they believe the person to be a friend or parent-like figure, and thus they may <u>fear</u> that if they report the abuse that their special relationship may end.

The abuser may also use threats and coercion once the abuse starts to suggest to the victim that no one will believe them or that the minor will be blamed for the abuse because they wanted it. As the abuser has also often groomed the victim's guardians and community, adults often trust the perpetrator and may not be suspicious of the grooming behaviors or changes in the child's behaviors.

The key to understanding grooming is that it is very hard to detect when it is happening as many of the grooming behaviors in and of themselves appear completely innocuous, and in many cases, they are. In fact, research shows that people are generally quite poor at identifying grooming behaviors before it is revealed that abuse has occurred. It is only in hindsight that the behaviors appear suspicious.

That is why it is especially important to know who is around your children and be aware of how they are interacting with your child. While this may result in you being an overly suspicious parent, it is always better to be safe than sorry. Many child-serving organizations that have had sex scandals that involved grooming like the Catholic Church and Boy Scouts, have now developed policies where children are not allowed to be alone with adults.

Similarly, by knowing about grooming practices, parents must keep the lines of communication with their children open and talk to them about these types of behaviors so that children know they can report anything to parents without fear of reprisal (Jeglic, E.L. (2019).

As Ms. Johnson heard the details of her son's abuse at the hands of her boyfriend, you could tell she was going to be physically sick. She started look haggard. Her eyes became very watery as tears began to drop down her weary face. Her almond complexion turned very pale. Her face looked like someone who was experiencing nausea and an upset stomach.

The therapist continued to give the details of the sexual abuse, according to Isaiah. Ms. Johnson's boyfriend raped Isaiah in the bushes behind the apartment complex. He raped Isaiah in the backseat of his car. He raped Isaiah in his bedroom. Ms. Johnson's boyfriend sodomized Isaiah by having anal sex with him and forced him to give and receive oral copulation. According to the therapist, Isaiah disclosed at least four different acts of sex on four different days.

After hearing all of this, Ms. Johnson got up and ran out of the room. She could not take listening to the details anymore. In her distress, Ms. Johnson did not notice the two small steps leading from the conference room—she tripped and fell. As the officers ran over to assist her, the tears continued to fall, and her cries became louder and louder. She began to scream out in pain. Emotional pain. Emotional pain that was turning into a physical reaction. The therapist got up to assist with calming her down. Just when it seemed like Ms. Johnson was calming down, controlling her breathing, she vomited all over the therapist. Everyone at the table got up to assist. Most of us had tears threatening to drop out, if not already flooding our eyelids. Once Ms. Johnson was escorted out of the room to clean herself up and get herself together, we all sat in silence around the table. No one spoke for the next ten to fifteen minutes, giving us time to gather our thoughts and emotions.

It truly was one of the saddest scenes I have experienced in my twenty-plus years working with children and families. This was the most heartbreaking sexual abuse case I had worked in my sixteen years in Child Welfare. I have worked on in most areas of the arena. I have worked as a Child Abuse Investigator, In-home Services Social Worker, Foster Care Supervisor, and as an Investigations Supervisor. Of all the cases I have worked or supervised in those sixteen years, I will forever remember Isaiah and Ms. Johnson.

Ms. Johnson's boyfriend was arrested and charged with several counts of Rape First Degree and Sodomy First Degree. He pled guilty and was sentenced to fifteen years in prison.

So, what happened to Isaiah? How did he get through this trauma? Isaiah remained in the in-patient treatment facility for the next six months. He received individual, specialized counseling for child victims of sexual abuse. Isaiah and Ms. Johnson received family counseling to work on their relationship and his transition back into the home. Ms. Johnson participated in group counseling for parents of sexually abused children. Both Ms. Johnson and Isaiah continued to receive mental health counseling and in-home services as he transitioned back into her home.

As you read this, you probably feeling sad, scared, and real protective of your young children. I know that after the first three months of working in this field, I was very protective of my son. I became hyperaware of his interactions with other people outside of my household. However, research shows that many child victims of sexual abuse are perpetrated by close friends or family members. Because of the many trainings I have attended and my on-the-job experiences, I started having conversations early with my son. We had the "good touch-bad touch-unwanted touch" conversations regularly. When I started in child welfare, my son was five years old, so he was old enough to have those conversations. I started those conversations even earlier with my granddaughter. As parents, it is our responsibility to protect our children to the *best of our abilities*. Every parent's ability is different. Despite all that I have seen in my sixteen years in Child Welfare, I believe that all parents genuinely love their children and want the best for them.

Dr. Elizabeth Jeglic also gives some concrete suggestions for parents to keep their kids safe:

1. Children should not go alone to outings/overnights with adults that are not immediate family members. If a child goes with a family member, then it is always best when more than one relative/child attends.

2. Minors with cell phones should not be receiving personal text messages or e-mails from adults in the community. If

a coach or teacher uses text messages for communication, the texts should be directed at the entire group of students or parents.

3. Do not encourage secret-keeping in your house. Explain to your child that if another adult tells them to keep a secret from their parent, that is wrong, and they should always let you know and that you will not be mad.

4. When developmentally appropriate, talk to your children about grooming behaviors and tell them that they should always tell you if anything another adult does makes them uncomfortable. Let them know that you will always believe them and take their concerns seriously.

5. Be wary of other adults that show special attention to your child. While coaches or teachers may choose to single out exceptional talent, it should be in the context of the activity and they should not be providing your child with gifts or treats that are not bestowed upon all children.

6. Be cautious of adults that touch your child unnecessarily. In some sporting activities, coaches may be required to touch the child to position their body or spot them, but let your child know that they should tell you if any adult is touching them in a way that makes them feel uncomfortable or doesn't listen when they ask them to stop.

Jeglic, E.L. (2019) What Parents Need to Know About Sexual Grooming. *Psychology Today*. Retrieved from https://www.psychologytoday.com/us/blog/protecting-children-sexual-abuse/201901/what-parents-need-know-about-sexual-grooming.

Working in Child Welfare, I investigated and worked on a range of different cases— such as the sexual abuse I just described, to drug abuse, to discipline issues, to something as simple, yet not so simple as a parent struggling financially and living in poverty, etc. Let me tell you about another case that I worked on early in my career.

I completed an investigation with allegations of neglect. Mrs. Thomas had physical custody of her three girls, ages four, six, and eight. The report came in that the middle child has belt marks on her back and leg. Upon interviewing the alleged victim child, she told me that her mom spanked her with a belt because she let her little sister run out in the street. I observed three linear red welts on the back of her leg. I interviewed Mrs. Thomas, and she confirmed that she did spank her daughter. She says the younger two kids were playing in the front yard, and the four-year-old ran into the street. She says the six-year-old was supposed to be watching her. Based on just those details, what do you think the underlying issue is? If you said supervision, you are correct. It was a case where Mrs. Thomas thought it was okay for her six-year-old child to supervise her four-year-old while she was in the house cleaning. She admitted to hitting her daughter with a belt three times. She says she was aiming for her behind, but her daughter kept squirming, so she hit her on the back and leg. Mrs. Thomas was not remorseful at all.

Even after discussing appropriate supervision, Mrs. Thomas did not think anything was wrong with her expectations of her children. Her lack of control and inappropriate discipline and leaving marks on her child were addressed by way of a Safety Plan–which Mrs. Thomas refused to acknowledge. Due to her refusal to sign the Safety Plan as required and her lack of understanding regarding supervision of her children and appropriate discipline, I placed the children with their father, Mr. Thomas. Mr. and Mrs. Thomas had been separated for three years. The kids had been in her physical custody since their separation. Mr. Thomas signed a Safety Plan agreeing to have appropriate supervision of the children at all times, no physical discipline pending the investigation, and the children were to have no unsupervised contact with their mother. Meaning, the children could not be with Mrs. Thomas without another adult there as well, supervising the contact.

Approximately one week after the children were placed with Mr. Thomas, I made a school visit to see the girls. The eight-year-old disclosed that her mother spanked her, and she showed me a bruise on her arm. It was a linear bruise, greenish blue in color, and looked like a ruler. I asked her when and where she saw her mother. She told me that she had seen her mother a few days ago. She said that her Daddy took them over to her mother's house while he went to work. The other two children confirmed they had been at their mother's house as well. Before I contacted Mr. Thomas, I consulted with my supervisor, and we consulted with the agency's attorney. It was decided that the children needed to be removed from Mr. Thomas due to the violation of the Safety Plan.

I reached out to Mr. Thomas and scheduled a home visit for that afternoon. My coworker and I met with him at his home. The girls were there. Upon entering the apartment, the girls ran to me and gave me a hug. They told their dad that I came to see them at school today. Mr. Thomas looked shocked. He looked like he was "caught" with his hand in the cookie jar. We sat down at the small round kitchen table. I asked the girls to go to their rooms while I spoke with their dad. Mr. Thomas looked concerned at this point. I explained that I had made a school visit and had spoken to the girls. As I looked at him, I felt bad knowing that I was planning to remove the girls from his home. This was the hard part of the job. It is not a good feeling to separate a family. It almost feels deceitful, entering someone's home with a smile. They are smiling back nervously at me. All the while, I know that I am getting ready to turn their smile into a frown and perhaps make them shed tears.

I asked Mr. Thomas if the girls had been to their mother's house. At first, he looked shocked at the question. Then, immediately, he came up with a story that he thought would sound good to me. Mr. Thomas told me that he took the girls over to their mother's house to visit. He was there as well. The girls asked for something to snack on, but their mother did not have any snacks. Mr. Thomas says he ran to the store to get the girls something to eat. He continued to explain that he did not think it would be a "big deal since the store was only ten minutes away."

"Mr. Thomas, do you have the Safety Plan that you signed?" My colleague was sitting next to me, observing the interview. She was a new worker. I took the original copy of the Safety Plan out of my folder.

Mr. Thomas nodded his head, "Yes."

"Do you remember the reason for the Safety Plan, Mr. Thomas?" I asked him as I thought back to the story the girls told me when I visited them at school. All three girls told me they were at their mother's house while their dad went to work.

Again, Mr. Thomas nodded his head yes. At that point, I asked him to explain the Safety Plan to me. He looked down and sighed. Since he did not speak up, I reminded him of the reason for the Safety Plan. I explained it the exact same way that I had explained it to him a week ago. After reviewing the signed Safety Plan and telling Mr. Thomas that his story isn't the same story that the girls told me, I asked him if he wanted to explain to me why the girls were at Mrs. Thomas. Finally, he told me the truth. Mr. Thomas explained the babysitter did not show up that day, and he had no one else to watch the girls while he went to work. He said he kept calling her, but she did not answer the phone, and it was too late for him to call into work to request the day off. He further explained that he was already on probation for calling off work too many times. So, he did what he felt was his only option–he took the girls to their mother while he went to work. I asked Mr. Thomas if he had any other support systems that could help him with the kids-family members, close friends, or anyone else. He stated he did not have anyone who was willing to assist him with the kids.

After staffing this case with my supervisor and the agency attorney, a decision was made to file a petition and remove the kids due to violation of the Safety Plan **and** the child being physically disciplined with visible bruising. Mr. Thomas was upset about the agency's decision. However, he also understood that he had no other support in caring for the kids. The children were placed in a foster home for three months. During this time, both Mr. and Mrs. Thomas successfully completed parenting classes. They participated in family counseling. The children went back home with Mrs. Thomas, and the parents shared custody. By this time, the case was closed, and Mr. and Mrs. Thomas had rekindled their relationship.

Why do I call this chapter "the calling?" Let me explain. As I explained earlier, my original major was Computer Science. I wanted to become a Computer Programmer. Math. Numbers. Business. Those are the areas where I showed my strongest skills. I was never a people person. In general, I did not like people. I wanted a career where I could work independently. Kids. Never liked them except for the ones in my family. I did not want to work with or around kids either. How did I go from Computer Science to Social Work? Nothing but GOD. I believe that GOD ordered my steps to fulfill the calling He has on my life. Computer Science to Business Management to Family Studies to Social Work. HE lined up my life in the order that was required. I worked in Family Court for about a year. I volunteered as a Support Counselor with the Bluegrass Rape Crisis Center for two years. I worked in Child Welfare for sixteen years. Today, I work as a School Social Worker. In every aspect of my life, God put me in place to work with children and families. I never wanted this calling. However, you know the saying, *"If you want to make God laugh, tell Him your plans."* Because He has the final say, I could do nothing but submit to His plans and Calling on my Life. I would not change anything about my career path. I absolutely love being a Social Worker. I absolutely love working with kids. I absolutely love working with families. Social Work. It is my calling, my passion, my life.

CHAPTER 9

THE TRANSITION

The Move

In December 2004, I graduated from the University of Kentucky with my Master's Degree in Social Work. I was a homeowner. My son was ten years old and in the fifth grade. He was a star baseball player for an Amateur Athletic Union (AAU) traveling team. He also played basketball and football. Life was good. I was still working for the Department of Social Services in Child Welfare. I was making decent money. Life was good. As good as life was for me, I wanted more. I wanted to move to a city with more people who looked like me. More blacks. More black professionals. Charlotte, North Carolina. My aunt and cousins had lived in Charlotte for over twenty years. I had been visiting the city for the last two years, and I always enjoyed myself. Charlotte was full of black professionals, so I decided to make that move. I put my house on the market for sale, and I transitioned to Charlotte in July of that year. I was excited as I made the move to Charlotte. I immediately found a job. I signed the lease on my apartment. I loved the city of Charlotte. Almost sixteen years later, I still love the Queen City.

As excited as I was about the move, that transition was tough on my son. He did not cope well with us moving to another state. At that time, I did not think about the negative impact the move would have on my son. I thought I was giving my son an opportunity to grow up in a city with more people who looked like him. I wanted to give him an opportunity to be in a city where professional people looked like him. I had a dream for my son, and I thought Charlotte was the answer. However, what I thought would be a positive move, turned out to have a negative effect on my son. Joel became depressed and discouraged. My initial thought was that he would "get over it" and get back to his normal self. That did not happen. Sure, he adjusted to the move. He continued to be active in sports. He continued to do well in school but not as well as before the move. Despite his adjusting, he continued to be depressed. His teachers would tell me that Joel is a great kid but appears to be discouraged. So, I allowed him to return to Kentucky for his sophomore year of high school. He moved back to Lexington and stayed with my aunt for a year. Allowing him to move back to Kentucky without me was one of the hardest decisions I have ever made. However, at the time, I felt like it was detrimental to his mental health. His depression never eased up. He did get involved in sports. He played baseball and basketball for his middle school team. In his freshman year of high school, he was the only freshman to make the varsity football team.

Joel's enthusiasm and participation in sports did not cover up his depression. He was angry that I moved him to Charlotte. He was angry that I took him from his cousins and Aunt Boo. He was angry that I took him away from his friends. He was angry that I took him away from his coaches. He was angry that I moved him away from Lexington, KY. He needed to be back with his family and friends. So, I let him move back. Fortunately, Joel decided on his own that he wanted to come back with his immediate family. At the end of his sophomore year, Joel came back to Charlotte. Joel was able to go back to what he "thought" he wanted and needed. Here is a letter from Joel that depicts his journey regarding his move back to Lexington:

Dear Mom

Let me share the experience I have deemed as "the transformation year," my sophomore year of high school. This is the year where everything began to become clear to me. After the move to Charlotte, NC, from Lexington, KY, I had a tough time adjusting to my new life. For years I attempted whatever I could to try to get back to my hometown, and after many failed attempts, success crept in. You finally allowed me the opportunity to go back home, and I took full advantage. I had made it up in my mind that this was the best thing for me. Filled with excitement, I called Aunt Sharon and asked if I could come back to Lexington and stay with them. She answered yes, and with no hesitation. I was on my way back to Lexington. Now I had struggled throughout middle school and my freshman year at Hopewell High School because I was still adjusting. So, for me to be moving back to Lexington, I was excited for what I thought was me getting my life back on track. However, that was not the case. Instead of getting back on track, the trouble that I had been looking for in NC was finding me in Kentucky. Yes, I was back around my family. Yes, I was back around my friends. Yes, I was back around old coaches and teammates, but that was not the solution.

Starting school in Lexington that year was like a dream come true for me. I was in love with the fact that not only was I in my hometown, but I was actually going to school with my closest cousins and friends. I made the football team and dominated as usual, and I was very popular around the school. However, with all the positive things going on, I still could not avoid the devil's work. Fight after fight, I could not seem to handle my anger any other way. Even with having exactly what I wanted and exactly what I asked, my life still was not in order. Things got worse and worse with every new fight/event; I was gaining new enemies and burning bridges. It finally got to a point where Uncle Mike had enough and eventually sent me back to North Carolina.

I bring up this experience because it was the beginning of my transformation to becoming a man. This experience alone started *the healing process, drove me to forgiveness, helped me understand the decision you made as a mother. Even from that year on, I had seen how bad Lexington was spiraling out of control. That experience helped me understand your intentions. It helped me to start thinking of this situation with logic and not emotion. With that being said, mom, I understand. When I returned to North Carolina, I returned with a different mindset. I was ready to be successful. I was ready to explore the opportunities that Charlotte had to offer. Most importantly, I was ready to make peace with my current situation and make the best of it. Who knows where my life would be without your guidance? At the end of the day, looking back, I can only thank you for giving me the best possible path to success the best way you knew how. I love you.*

Sincerely,

Your Son, A Motivated Black Man!

It wasn't until recently that I learned the depth of his pain and grief with the move from Lexington to Charlotte. We had started family counseling, just he and I, to work on our communication with one another. When the therapist asked him about his deepest anger, he immediately revisited the move. As we participated, from two different households, in a Zoom counseling session, I thought back to the look on my son's face the day we left Lexington. My little cousin and Joel's best friend,

Daron, stayed with us the last two nights before we packed up the U-Haul and left for a new life. The way Joel and Daron cried when they had to be pulled apart after saying goodbye was gut-wrenching. Imagine two nine-and ten-year-old children who have been best friends/cousins since birth. Joel and Daron grew up together. Daron, the oldest by nine months, was like my second son. I was in the delivery room when he was born. I watched, with tears in my eyes, as Daron was born. Not knowing that I was pregnant at the time, I remember thinking that I couldn't wait to experience such a miracle. One month later, I found out that I was pregnant. After Joel was born, Daron and Joel were inseparable. Due to them being so close in age, my aunt and I did everything together when it came to the boys. They grew up close and called each other brothers. Needless to say, when we moved six and one-half hours away, it was detrimental to both of them.

Joel's emotions and feelings around the decision I made to move to Charlotte is documented here in a Dear Mom Letter:

Dear Mom,

From the time I was old enough to understand my existence in this world, I was a perfectionist. I wanted to be the absolute G.O.A.T (Greatest of All Time), and there was no unique area I wanted to be the best at everything. I figured that if I went exactly by what society deemed perfect that I would be successful in my goal. As a child, everything I did, I took seriously. I gave my maximum effort and emotion. I put my heart into it. From school to sports, to making friends, to being the best son, cousin, nephew, grandchild, etc. I wanted to be the best. I wanted to be everyone's favorite person, and I was making moves to be that. I felt like I was in the perfect position in life. I had everything going for me.

Throughout elementary school, I knew how smart I was, and my grades reflected, even gaining me an academic achievers award. Within those years, I had become a star in baseball, a star in football, and an above-average basketball player in my hometown. I had big dreams of one day becoming a professional athlete and being a successful black man in America. I had grown extremely close to my family, and I loved being in their presence. I also had many friends, a few who were really close to me that I had been around most of my life. In my mind, nothing could go wrong, and then it happened.

The move at the time was one of the worst days of my life. The only thing that gave me a slight bit of comfort was that Daron was coming with us for a while. I was all right initially moving in and settling, but once Daron went back, reality set in, and everything went downhill. I was exhausted with emotions—anger, sadness, depression. I did not know what else to do, so I resulted to being rebellious. I decided to take a path that I was always against. First starting with school because I knew the level of importance you placed on my education. Even though I knew how smart I was, I wanted to hide it. I decided not to participate in class, projects, or complete homework, thinking this would get your attention. Secondly, I decided that I would start fighting all the time and join a gang. I watched my life begin to crash while I created the motion of the movie. As time moved forward, the consequences of my actions started to kick in. In particular, I was not able to play sports my ninth-grade year all because of a poor GPA.

Eventually, I was blessed with the opportunity to go back to Lexington. Ironically, I could not hit the switch, so I continued to stay in trouble to the point my Uncle had to make me leave and go back to Charlotte. It was in those spiraling moments I began to realize it was not about my location. It was a personal issue, something I had to work on internally. With the way things were going in Lexington, my life would have definitely continued down the wrong path. This made me appreciate your decision so much more. It helped me realize your intentions. I sat back, analyzed your thought process, and appreciated it.

At the end of it all, I realized that I did nothing but set myself back with my actions. It was not purposely; it is just the way my immature mind was thinking. I began to forgive you at that point. However, in all actuality, you had nothing to be sorry about. You made a decision. As your child, I will always need you. To this day, I still call you if I need something. You gave me the confidence to believe in you. I should have never second-guessed your decision. I should have made the best out of the *opportunities you presented me. For that, I would like to apologize and ask for your forgiveness and let you know that you gave me no reason to doubt you. I look back, being the man I am today, and I have you to thank for it. No regrets because I am thankful for the entire process of becoming me. I am still on that journey. Life is real, and with no cheat codes or shortcuts, I am making a way.*

Sincerely, More than a Statistic!

The Meet & Marriage

Let me take you back to the beginning of our new life in a new city and state.

My sister and I decided to go out for a night of music and drinks. I picked her up from her place, and we headed out with no destination planned. We were driving down Albemarle Road when we spotted a parking lot with lots of cars and music blasting. I turned my tan Chrysler into the parking lot and looked for a spot to park. After driving around the parking lot a few times, we finally saw a park pulling out and waited to pull into its spot. While freshening up our faces in the car mirrors, we could hear the vibes of the music playing. We were excited to get out for a night on the town. We walked inside the sports bar. After waiting in line for ten minutes, we were seated at a tabletop close to the back. The back of the sports bar housed a club.

Even though we are seven years apart, my sister and I were both satisfied with the mix of music. The DJ was playing some old school and some new school. My sister and I began to order drinks and appetizers. The bar kept messing up our drinks, so they had to make us new drinks. After about an hour, we had enjoyed two to three drinks each. I was feeling good that night. I was relaxed and enjoying the scene. As the night progressed, I disclosed a very personal experience to my sister. After hearing my story, she became emotional and began to cry. My sister has always been very emotional. Her response caused me to become emotional, but I refused to shed a tear. I had learned in my life to be hard, guarded, and hide my emotions.

There was a bouncer working the door of the club. Nice body. Dark skin. Bald head. I saw him. He saw us. He kept looking over at our table. I guess the sight of two drunk women, one crying hysterically, is enough to cause concern to the bouncer at the club. I saw him coming to the table. He looked concerned. He walked up to our table and said, "Is she okay? Do you all need anything?" My first reaction was to look down at his hands. They were ashy. I took my lotion out of my purse and began to rub it on his hands. After the hand rub down, we learned each other's names and exchanged phone numbers. As the night progressed, he continued to check on my sister and me. We all made small conversation for the rest of the night. And so, my story begins.

I was new to Charlotte by way of Kentucky. I moved to Charlotte in July 2005, and I met my now ex-husband, Ronnie, in March 2006. We met on a Saturday night. We had our first date the following Monday. Tuesday, he came to my house and never left. Seriously. Sounds crazy, right? My son woke up the next day and was surprised to see Ronnie asleep on our couch. From that day on, we stayed together every day. The only exception was when I went to Kentucky or when he went to his hometown of Laurinburg. He continued to keep his apartment, and I had my own apartment for the next two years. However, we always stayed together. Although we were inseparable, we did not spend a lot of "quality" time together. He was working three jobs. He was busy working day and night. I remember when he confessed that he wanted us to be committed and work on a relationship. I told him that day, "You don't have time for me." Little did I know that I would repeat that same statement several times over the next eleven years.

Year after year after year, I made that same statement. Yet, I married him to have a companion. It doesn't make sense, or does it? I wanted a partner to enjoy life and grow old together. I wanted to have someone that I could count on to enjoy dinner, movies, or bowling. I wanted to have someone to walk through the park with me or around the lake. I wanted a partner to spend quality time with and connect intimately, emotionally, and mentally. I wanted a partner to travel and explore the world.

As I reflect on why I got married, I often wonder why I married for companionship and not for love. Yes, you read it correctly. I married for companionship. Did I love my husband? Absolutely! However, love was not the underlying reason I accepted his marriage proposal. He proposed three times before I accepted his proposal. Being a girl who never dreamt of getting married, I was not sold on a fantasy of love and happily ever after. I always felt that love is important and vital in a relationship but not the sole reason for marriage. Today, I feel very differently.

So why did I marry my ex-husband? I was a single mother of a ten-year-old when I met him. I was college-educated with a few degrees. I had worked in state government since I finished my undergraduate degree in 1997. I had been on my own since I was nineteen. I was a strong woman. I was independent. I took care of myself and my son with little to no help from his father. However, I was tired of doing it alone. I often wondered what it felt like to be able to "just be" instead of being all. I wanted a companion. I wanted someone who I could depend on "if" I needed him. Therefore, I married him to have a companion. We married on April 4, 2009.

For many years, my marriage was great! The newlywed years, as they call them, were refreshing and exciting! As the years passed by and we became empty-nesters, things began to change. I quickly realized the one thing that I married for, "companionship," was the one thing I felt was lacking from my marriage. Yes, my husband loved me, cared for me, provided for me, and desired me. Nevertheless, I did not have what I wanted or needed, his time.

My husband was addicted to work. I did not recognize it as an addiction early on in our relationship. The nonstop working was already spinning when I met him. At that time, he was working three jobs. As our relationship started to grow and he wanted a commitment, I told him that he did not have time for a commitment. He initially thought I was joking. I pointed out to him that he was too busy to develop a real relationship with me or anyone else. Over time, when I would make that comment, he would say, "I'll make time." That response became a running record in our home. However, I gave it the benefit of the doubt and assumed things would change. Three years later, we got married. Things still had not changed. Between my full-time job and his full-time job plus two part-time jobs, we hardly spent any "quality time" together. Yes, my husband loved me, cared for me, provided for me, and desired me.

For the first year, our time together was limited. We had two boys that were busy with sports–football, basketball, baseball, and track. Matt, my bonus son, came to live with us a year before we got married. He is one year younger than Joel. Because I was so busy with the boys, I did not focus on the fact that my husband was working all the time. I sucked it up. I rationalized him working all the time by thinking that I did not have time for him either. His work schedule eventually became a problem in terms of him attending the boys' sporting events. I would be angry that he did not make the sacrifice to be at the games as opposed to working. To me, it was a no-brainer. Your boys are playing sports. As a parent, you make the sacrifice, and you are there for every single game. However, he was not. I rationalized it by thinking that we needed the extra money to take care of the boys and pay for all their extracurricular expenses. Again, I sucked it up.

By 2014, both boys had graduated and moved out of the house. That is when my eyes opened up to the Empty Nest Syndrome–it is very real! The feeling of loneliness that took over me was unexplainable. I knew that the boys kept me busy. My son has played sports since he was four years old. It all started with T-ball, then baseball, basketball, football, and track– it was year-round sports, so I was used to being busy. Honestly, my son's schedule is what gave me life. I did manage to get some time in there because I started traveling when he was young. However, most of my time was spent traveling for my son's sports. When my bonus son came into my life, the rest of my time went to him. He also played sports and was sometimes on a different team than my son. Being a mother was my life, my purpose. Being a parent is what I did well. Very well. Another symptom of the Empty Nest Syndrome that was particularly hard for me was the feeling of losing control. The boys were adults now. They no longer lived in my house. They no longer had to report their every move to me. I no longer had control over what time they came home or how they spent their money. Yes, Empty Nest Syndrome is real!

Being an empty nester, I no longer spent all of my extra time at sporting events. I simply had "extra time." It was during this time I realized how much time I spent alone. Because I had nothing to do with my extra time, I realized how much my husband was away from home. By this time, he was working his full-time job, doing security Thursday-Sunday evenings, and doing other odd jobs–detailing cars, moving people, etc. He eventually bought a party bus, too. My husband was what I called a "legal hustler." He did a little bit of everything to make money. It was as if he could not and would not sit still. If he ever had any free time, he would make up some work to do. Security brought him home in the wee hours of the night. I went to bed alone. I woke up alone. I was always ALONE. ALONE. It hit me like a brick. Damn, Deleisha, you are always by yourself. You are always ALONE. Yes, my husband loved me, cared for me, provided for me, and desired me.

When I say I went to bed by myself and woke up by myself, I do not mean that he stayed out all night. He never did that. My husband always came home. He just did not require much sleep. He would get home around 3:00 a.m. after working security at the club, and he would be back up and moving by 7:00 a.m. No, he did not have a job that required him to be at work by 7:00 a.m. He would get up and detail cars or help someone move or go look for work. Sometimes he would just be "working" in the garage doing whatever he could to keep busy. When working in the garage, it was like he wasn't home. Yes, my husband loved me, cared for me, provided for me, and desired me.

My husband was never home. I began to feel empty. That feeling caused me to become insecure in my marriage. I started to wonder if he was out cheating on me and not working. I started to wonder if maybe he was seeing a woman at the club where he worked. As months turned to years, those questions began to consume me. When he was gone, I could not stop wondering if he was with other women. Insecurity overtook me. I began to question myself as his wife. Was he sexually satisfied? Was I not paying him enough attention? Was I nagging him too much about staying home? Is he no longer attracted to me? Once the insecurities started, they became a rolling ball that never ended. Like a snowball, my insecurities grew from the size of a tennis ball to the size of a basketball. My once very secure, strong, and confident persona quickly diminished. Yes, my husband loved me, cared for me, provided for me, and desired me.

Did I address it? Absolutely. Month after month. Year after year. I expressed my feelings of loneliness to my husband. I can remember crying to him and begging him to stay home and not go to work some nights. Every year for our anniversary, we took a trip. During that trip, we would talk about how we could improve our marriage. We talked about what we needed or wanted more of from each other. I always expressed that I felt alone and lonely. I always asked him to establish a balance between work and home. He would make some immediate provisions. The provisions would last for a week or two, and then he would fall right back into his routine of constantly working. Yes, my husband loved me, cared for me, provided for me, and desired me.

I asked him to go to counseling. First, he agreed. I made appointments for us, and he would come up with an excuse about why he could not make it. Eventually, he flat out said he wouldn't go to counseling. I finally accepted the fact that my husband was a workaholic. I looked it up on Wikipedia: Workaholic. "A workaholic is a person who works **compulsively**. The person works at the cost of their sleep, meeting friends or family. While the term generally implies that the person enjoys their work, it can also alternately imply that they **simply feel compelled** to do it. There is no generally accepted medical definition of such a condition, although some forms of stress, impulse control disorder, obsessive-compulsive personality disorder, and obsessive-compulsive disorder can be work-related. Much like alcoholism as a form of an alcoholic but in terms of work, therefore a workaholic."

As I read the definition of a workaholic, there is one word that repeatedly shouts out to me. **Compulsively.** My husband worked at the cost of his sleep and his family. He has worked more than one job since the day I met him. Even when he wasn't officially "at work," he was still working. He would detail cars. He would help people move. He would help other people do their work. I have been asking my husband to make time for me since we got married. I have repeatedly asked, no, begged him to make time for me. I can remember all the times that I'd sit him down to discuss my concerns. I would express to him that I need him. I would tell him that I need my husband home with me. I expressed my disappointment about him missing the boys' sporting events because he was working. Football, basketball, baseball. He missed many games over the years because he was "working." I didn't expect him to stop working altogether. What I expected was that he would balance work and home. My husband did not have to work all the time to make ends meet. He had me. I was his wife. We were supposed to be a team. My husband **simply felt compelled** to work all the time. He has explained to me that work is all he knows. He has explained that he has worked his entire life, and no one has ever given him anything.

Just like any other addiction, the effect on our marriage was devastating. Neglect. I felt like my husband neglected my needs– emotionally, mentally, and physically. It was hard for us to maintain an emotional connection because we did not spend quality time together. Our time together was hit or miss. The mental connection was lacking because we lost the emotional connection. The physical connection was never an issue, but that's all it was. Physical Sex. After years of feeling neglected and unwanted by my husband, I checked out. I no longer felt any connection with him. I always loved my husband; I just didn't feel connected to him any longer. Yes, my husband loved me, cared for me, provided for me, and desired me. My husband didn't know how to love me the way I desired to be loved.

My #1 love language has always been *Quality Time*. Did my husband make time for me? Sure. Once a week, we had a date night. It usually was the same routine. Dinner and a movie. My husband thought spending physical time with me once a week was enough. What he was missing was the "Quality" of his time. Our date nights were always limited to certain days and hours because he would have to go to work. We never had date nights on the weekends because he was always working security–Day parties as well as Night parties. On our weekday date night, my husband had to leave for work by 7:00 p.m. So that left little time for me. Our time together always felt rushed. On the rare occasions that we did have a date on the weekend, his phone was constantly ringing. Club owners were calling for security. He answered. Then he would call his team to go work security at the clubs. Friends were calling. He answered. Anybody called. He answered. The "lack of quality" time I received from him felt more like an obligation than a desire to spend time with me.

Our time together was very seldom "Quality." According to Gary Chapman, author of the book, *The 5 Love Languages*, "Just because two people are in the same place together, doesn't mean they're actually spending quality time with one another. Hence, the "quality" component of this love language. The important thing to know is that it's more about the level of attention paid to your partner than it is about how many minutes or hours you spend by their side."

Ironically, my husband's love language, based on the quiz, was Quality Time. He expressed that he wanted to spend time with me. He expressed that he liked to spend time with me. We were both wanting and desiring quality time. However, we were obviously, never on the same page about what "*quality time*" looks like. What do you think about this situation? Is it possible that we both wanted the same thing, but the delivery looked different? At the time, I didn't feel he wanted to spend time with me. The time we did spend together didn't feel genuine. It felt like he was doing things with me because that's what *I* wanted. Not because he wanted it.

How did I cope?

I threw myself into taking vacations. I took vacations out of the country. I took beach trips. I took road trips. I took trips across the country. I jumped on board with anything that gave me some attention and time. My husband never said a word. He never told me not to go. He never told me that we did not have the money to go. He never acted or appeared to be upset or angry over me leaving. His acceptance or lack of emotion about me constantly being on the go just added to my insecurities. In my mind, I felt like he wanted me to leave, so he did not have to hear me complain about him always working. I could not grasp the idea that my husband had *no* problem with me always being gone. All I wanted was for him to tell me not to go. I wanted to hear my husband say he missed me and needed me to stay home. I never heard any of that. There were times when I felt like he wanted me gone so he could be with other women. No matter how much I thought about it, I could not understand it.

Today, I do not believe that to be true. I do not believe he had other women that he was entertaining. I can remember New Year's Eve about two years before we separated. We were eating at my favorite restaurant, On the Border. I wanted us to have a serious talk about my feelings. I said to him, "I'm not going into 2016 like this with you. I will not be lonely in our marriage for another year." I was angry and hurt when I said this to him. I wanted him to understand me and tell me everything was going to be okay. I wanted so badly for him to tell me that he would make the changes and spend more time at home.

Instead, my husband started crying, and he talked about how hard he worked to provide for our family. He was saying that he wanted me to be able to take vacations and go shopping. He told me that he wanted me to have everything I wanted. He continued to cry as he told me that sometimes he would be hurting so bad from his back injury, but he still went to work for me. For us. For our family. As I listened to my husband explain his reasoning for working ALL the time, and I watched him cry, I felt bad. I felt so sorry that he felt like he had to work even in pain just to provide for our family.

However, I also felt like he was not listening to me at that moment, and he did not understand my feelings. By this time, in year seven of our marriage, I had told him several times that I would rather have him at home with me than to have his money. I had told my husband that "we" are a team, and where he lacked financially, I could step in. I made a decent salary. I could make up the difference, and I wanted to pick up the difference. That would mean that my husband could cut back on his hours and spend more time at home. I craved his attention and his time. I craved intimacy with him. I craved to be fulfilled mentally, emotionally, and physically. By physical, I do not mean sex. Sex was never an issue in our marriage. Sex was the one thing he always made time for.

The Final Straw

I was preparing to leave for a twelve-day vacation in California with a girlfriend. Our flight was leaving at 8:30 the following morning. The day before I left, my husband and I had spent the day with family. We enjoyed quality time with family and friends. We cooked hamburgers, ribs, steak, and hot dogs on the grill. We listened to music. We talked. We laughed. The day felt so perfect. The sun was shining bright, and the temperature was in the lower 80's. As we drove back to our house, I felt emotional and excited because I was going to spend the rest of the evening with my husband before leaving for vacation. That feeling was short-lived. As we were driving home, his phone rang, and he answered. This is all I heard, "I'm headed home now. I just need to change, and I'll be there." Immediately, my eyes stung with tears. I could not believe I'd just heard my husband say he was going to work the night before my 12-day trip. I looked at him and asked if he was going to work. He looked at me and did not answer. I knew he didn't respond because he didn't want the argument. However, his lack of response was enough for me. The next morning, he drove me to the airport. We hugged. We kissed. I enjoyed California for the next twelve days.

Day 12-8:45 pm. As my flight landed, my stomach was a ball of excitement. After being away from my husband for twelve days, I could not wait to see him. I missed him. I missed his touch. I missed his smile. I missed his laugh. All I wanted to do was to fall into his arms. Sure, we talked every day I was gone, but I missed his physical presence so much. I had even forgotten the pain I felt before I left. My husband picked me up and greeted me with a BIG hug and kiss. We got in the car and headed home. Before we were off the airport property, his phone rang. He answered, "Yes, I'm coming. I just picked my wife up from the airport. I'll be there after I take her home. I have two other guys coming to work as well."

I felt like I had been sucker-punched in my chest. I remember thinking this has to be a joke. I looked at him, waiting for him to say I didn't hear what I had just heard him say. Immediately, my eyes stung with tears. When he didn't respond, the tears fell. My entire body felt a pain I didn't recognize. My heart hurt. My stomach hurt. My head hurt. I could no longer control my emotions. I began to cry uncontrollably. All I thought about was my husband doesn't love me. He doesn't want me. He does not want this marriage. That day, at that time, I knew I could no longer continue to be second to his work. He needed his work. I needed him. That night, I expressed to him I was unhappy and could not live in that feeling anymore. It wasn't the first time I had said those words to him. But it was the last. My husband looked at me with tears running down his face. He told me that he loves me, but he doesn't know how to make me happy, and he wants me to be happy.

We separated the following month. One year later, we divorced.

In hindsight, we could have made our marriage work. It would have required us both to do the work. I was willing. He was not. When I think about it, maybe I didn't love my husband the way he desired to be loved. Not maybe. I did not love him the way he desired to be loved. He needed to feel supported in all of his endeavors of work–the party bus, car detailing, and so on. Right or wrong, it was hard for me to support the things that took time away from me. I needed his time, his quality time. I needed his attention. Work endeavors took that quality time away from me. Why would I support those things? Because I was his wife. I wanted to be supportive. I did try to be supportive. I tried to encourage him and be a fan of his business endeavors. But ultimately, I could not support the things that made me unhappy.

CHAPTER 10

EVOLVING

For the last two years, I didn't feel like I had evolved. I didn't feel like I had healed. I felt like a failure because my marriage ended in divorce. Then I had an "affair" with my ex-husband. From March 2019-November 2019, I allowed myself to become involved physically with him. Because my heart had not healed, and I didn't have closure, I easily and comfortably fell in place being with him. I was so angry for giving myself to him for those eight months. During that time, I realized that being with him brought back those same feelings of insecurity and loneliness. It took me falling into a state of depression for me to realize I deserved something better from him or any other man. He didn't want to rekindle our relationship. He didn't want to work on our issues. To rekindle our relationship and work on our issues were the things I wanted. Because the communication was lacking, we never actually had a discussion about what we were doing during that time. I made the assumption that because we started being intimate again, we would work on rekindling our relationship. I made the assumption that my ex-husband wanted me back in his life because he was still in love with me. I thought he wanted more than just sex. Wrong. What I finally realized is that he wanted to have sex with me. He wanted to keep that physical connection with me. Nothing more, nothing less. He did not want to rekindle our relationship, our marriage. It wasn't until December 2019 that I accepted and owned my situation. That's when I truly started to evolve.

When I think about it, I feel like that brief "affair" was a necessary process that helped me to evolve and heal. Today, I no longer desire to be romantically involved with my ex-husband. I no longer long for his attention. I no longer wait for his phone calls. I choose Me. I recognize that I am deserving of a man's complete love. I was worthy of his complete attention, his complete commitment to me, and our relationship. Because I am evolving, I know my worth. I know what I want and need from a man. I am not willing to settle for anything that doesn't feel good. Even if it feels good, if it isn't completely satisfying for me, then I don't want it. I will not allow myself to be in a relationship where I feel lonely, ashamed, embarrassed, or unworthy of love.

Reflection

In an earlier chapter, I disclosed that I was sexually abused as a child. Once I started to remember the details of the incidents, I started to understand why I've been so guarded in my life; why I have this "wall" up that no one can penetrate. For a long time, I didn't understand where my emotions were coming from. Many of the emotions that I've felt and displayed are long-term effects of childhood sexual abuse. According to the American College of Obstetricians and Gynecologists, "Depression, anxiety, and anger are the most commonly reported emotional responses to childhood sexual abuse." As I disclosed in earlier chapters, anxiety, depression, and anger are emotions I have struggled with all my adulthood.

What I learned from my childhood sexual abuse was not to trust anyone to love me. I learned I needed to guard my heart so that no one could hurt me again. My abuser is a family member. He should have protected me, not hurt me. I trusted him. I trusted those around me to protect me. That did not happen. As I transitioned into adulthood, I did not allow myself to open up and be vulnerable with anyone. I've never completely trusted anyone. The easiest way for me to avoid being vulnerable was to keep love out of my commitment and marry for companionship. Companionship gave me what I "thought" I wanted in my marriage. But it didn't give me what I ultimately "needed" in my marriage.

Growing up with a drug-addicted Daddy has made a huge impact on my life. Again, I have a hard time trusting people to be genuine with me. I question everyone who comes into my life. My mind always wonders to several questions, *"What does he/she want from me? What is it I have that you want? Is this person* *being honest with me? Is this person trying to manipulate me?"*I know that my Daddy loves me and would do anything for me. However, I also know that he will steal from me, lie to me, and manipulate me to satisfy his addiction. But I do understand that is his addiction, not him!

My childhood traumas taught me two things: 1) I want to feel loved completely and unconditionally, and 2) Don't trust anyone to protect and love me. Yes, they are a contradiction of each other. Sounds weird, huh? It sounds weird even to me, but it's my truth. I'm working on number two. I know I have to trust in order to have an authentic, loving relationship.

Would I consider getting married again? Absolutely! I love the union of marriage. I love family. I love spending time with my family and surrounding myself with the love of my family. However, the next time around, I will approach it differently. I will be different before I enter the union of marriage. I want my next marriage to feel different. I want it to be different. I wish that my marriage could have lasted "until death do us part." But it didn't. There are so many things that we both could have done differently. But we didn't. We did not put in the work required to sustain the marriage. I love my ex-husband. My ex-husband loves me. We didn't know how to love together.

CHAPTER 11

THE RESOLUTION (COVID 19)

When God has a plan for you, and you do not listen, He has a way of making you listen. He has a way of silencing you. That is exactly what this public health crisis did to the world. God shut us all down. He silenced the world. He silenced me.

Coronavirus. COVID 19. Businesses closed. People lost their jobs. The Governor of North Carolina stopped in-person learning and implemented remote learning. Kids were no longer in a physical school building. Many people started working remotely. Everything shut down. The entire nation shut down. Here in NC, we went into a "Stay at Home Order," as did many other states. Nine months later, the entire world remains in a public health crisis. I'm still working remotely, and kids continue to receive remote learning. COVID positive cases have sky-rocketed, and the number of deaths from COVID-19 are unbelievable. Many people have lost loved ones to COVID-19. As I write, I have a close loved one who is currently in the hospital and on a ventilator after being diagnosed with COVID-19 and pneumonia. He continues to fight for his life.

As the pandemic hit the nation, I had my own pandemic that took over my life. The effects of the pandemic looked different to everyone. For me, it was a time of "self-discovery" and "healing work." My healing began before the country went into a pandemic. I was already in counseling. I had been seeing my therapist for about six months at that time. The most recent work with my therapist was healing from my divorce. After having a seven-month "affair" with my ex-husband, I was finally ready to do the work to heal from my divorce. I had a complete breakdown during one of my sessions. It was the first time I had shown sincere emotions about my marriage and divorce—about my ex-husband. This is where my work truly began.

My therapist gave me a book to work through, *The Fresh Start Divorce Recovery Workbook (Burns and Whiteman, 1992),* which helped me to understand and process the stages of grief as they related to my divorce. The book outlines the grieving process using a Crisis Timeline, also called The Slippery Slope. According to the book, "There are stages of divorce recovery. Divorce requires a grievance process, and the process typically takes at least two years. Divorce recovery is a process. You will have setbacks. It is not wrong to be at any particular point during the grieving process."

Stage 1-Denial: I was past the stage of denial. I remember my first encounter with denial. It was after a conversation with a close friend that I learned my husband was looking for an apartment. It was a month after my return from California. We were still living in the house together but not sleeping in the same bed. My husband was out looking at apartments after *he* decided that we needed to separate. In my mind, I thought it was just something that was said but not going to happen—until that day. Even though we had talked about the idea of separation, I was still in denial. I thought to myself, *"It will never happen to me.* We will make our marriage work." After working through the initial denial and moving into the other stages of divorce recovery, I found myself back in the denial stage several times over the last few years. Denial has helped me to move towards acceptance. *"Is denial wrong? No. It's a natural and necessary first step in the grieving process. It provides us with the time we need to prepare for what comes next."*

Stage 2-Anger: I have moved in and out of anger many, many times. Angry at myself. Angry at my ex-husband. Angry at the world—as if the world caused my divorce. I was angry that I got married in the first place. I was angry my marriage ended in divorce. I was angry because I felt like a failure. I felt like I failed my boys. I felt like I failed my family. I felt like I failed God. Angry. At times, my anger was displayed in fits of rage. I would get into fits of rage and throw things across the room. Scream to the top of my lungs. Flip out on my (at that time) husband and be mean and nasty to him for no reason. My burst of rage did nothing to solve my problem; it tended to make me angrier. Burns and Whiteman say, *"Rage is certainly one way of venting your emotions, but it can just make you angrier until you've lost control."*

Repression is my likeliest form of anger. Instead of venting my anger, I held it inside. Instead of being honest about how I was doing or feeling, I would simply put on my mask, smile, and say, "I'm fine." But, in reality, I was crushed. I was losing my mind. I felt like my life was over. Burns and Whiteman state, *"Repression may seem like a better option than rage, but in the long run, it can be just as destructive."*

Over time, I got to a point where I was able to display anger by way of redirection. I started to journal and write on a regular basis. I was able to take my anger energy and invest it in something positive. Journaling my thoughts and feelings was a way to express my anger without taking it out on my ex-husband. Earlier this year, I started working on my first book, *Evolve: From Heart Breaks to Hearts Healed.* Redirection was and still is my most productive way of displaying my anger. Writing and journaling are still my "go-to" release today. The goal was to display my anger by coming to a resolution. I was able to do that. My ex-husband and I were able to sit down and have civil conversations. I was able to acknowledge my wrongs and ask for his forgiveness for those things. He did the same. Resolution.

Stage 3-Bargaining: My brief affair with my ex-husband was my bargaining tool. I just wanted a solution to my pain, to my anger. What better solution than to reconnect with him? One year and four months after our last sexual encounter, I decided I would continue seeing and being intimate with my ex-husband. It felt good to be with him again. It felt natural. I missed him so much. Being with him took away my pain and my anger. Bargaining was temporary for us. It didn't take long for those old feelings of insecurity and lack of emotional connection to find their way back into my head and my heart. I was still lonely. Our affair only lasted for eight months. *"True reconciliation requires changes in attitudes and behavior."* This was my second time visiting this stage. Just one short month after we separated, my husband was coming to my apartment on a regular basis. He started spending the night at my apartment and in my bed several days a week. He had a key to my apartment. At that time, we were both bargaining to stop the pain. We wanted to get back to what we knew. We loved each other. We were comfortable with each other. We were good together—until I realized that there was no change in attitudes or behaviors.

Stage 4-Depression: As I think back over my marriage, my bouts of depression occurred before the separation. When I felt hopeless about whether my marriage would last, I would go into a depressed state. When I would cry over the realization that my needs were not being met in my marriage, I would go into a depressed state. When I thought about leaving my husband, I would go into a depressed state. At that time, depression looked a lot different for me. I threw myself into traveling and shopping as much as possible. It was the realization that my marriage was not going to work. After the separation and ultimately the divorce, my depression looked more like withdrawal. I withdrew from my family and friends. I didn't want to spend time with anyone, not even my granddaughter, I only had one at that time. I felt sad all the time. But I wore The Mask. I cried all the time in private. But I wore The Mask in public. I kept to myself and didn't reach out to anyone. My lifestyle became "depression." I went to work. I came home. I watched a little television. I went to bed. I was diagnosed with Seasonal Depression and Anxiety. I have spent many, many days, nights, and months in this stage. I've experienced this stage several times since my initial separation over three years ago. I must admit this is the stage I have visited the most. It was also in this stage I sought help and started my journey in therapy. *"It is during this stage when many people seek help after they have finally exhausted their efforts. Another positive aspect of depression is the self-examination that often occurs. Up to this stage, the focus is on everyone else."*

Stage 5-Acceptance: So many times, I thought I was in the acceptance stage. I was wrong. Something would happen, or someone would say something that would send me back into a different stage of grief. I finally moved out of depression by seeking help and doing the self-work. I learned to accept and be okay with whatever state of mind I am experiencing. I have

THE FACE BEHIND THE MASK

learned that it is okay to be angry or depressed. It is okay to feel denial. It is not okay to stay in those stages. *"The key to recovery is making wise decisions now about how you're going to live and what you are going to believe about yourself."* I no longer feel guilty about the way my marriage ended. I no longer feel guilty about the decisions, right or wrong, that were made during my marriage. I no longer feel guilty about disappointing God. He knows that I am not perfect. I am a work in progress.

According to Burns and Whiteman, "These five stages do not necessarily occur in the order presented. There is usually a general progression from denial through anger, bargaining, and depression, to acceptance, but each person moves through the process in a unique way. You might jump from denial to depression and then slip back to anger. It wouldn't be unusual for you to go through all five stages in the same day."

Forgiveness is the final stage on the Crisis Timeline (The Slippery Slope). Looking back through my book, I noticed I dated my state of forgiveness as February 23, 2020. That's almost one year ago. Today, I'm still forgiving. I forgive myself for making bad decisions. I forgive myself for not being understanding enough. I forgive myself for not being supportive enough. I forgive myself for having to go through the process. I forgive my ex-husband for his part in our marriage and divorce. Today, my ex-husband and I are in a great space. We stay in contact because we genuinely care about one another. Although we don't have biological kids together, we share our kids and grandbabies. We keep each other updated about the boys and grandbabies, as well as my other three bonus children and grandkids. Most importantly, we forgive one another, and we are able to remain friends. We were together for twelve years, married for nine years.

Once I was able to go through the steps of the grieving process and be at peace with my divorce, my work began around other areas in my life. I have been addressing anxiety, depression, and avoidance issues during psychotherapy. I've completed assignments and work regarding emotional blockage, forgiveness for myself and others, avoidance, and codependency. I have done my work. I will continue to do my work. For me, that's what has worked and continues to work for me. I do my work. I can't grow as a person without addressing my issues and the secrets that have kept me stuck. I am no longer stuck. I no longer have secrets. I no longer wear the Mask. Here I am. This is Deleisha Webb without the Mask.

As I reflect over my life, I have no regrets. Would I have done a few things differently? Hmmm... maybe. I am a firm believer everything happens for a reason. I accept the things that have happened in my life. I have very few regrets. My life experiences have shaped me into the woman I am today. Over the last three years since my separation and divorce, and through this process of self-work, I have learned more about myself than I learned during my entire adult years. Today, I am whole. I am complete. I am happy being Me! No Filters! No Mask!

REFERENCES

ACOG.org. "Adult Manifestation of Childhood Sexual Abuse." *The American College of Obstetricians and Gynecologists.* Accessed January 2021. https://www.acog.org/clinical/clinical-guidance/committee-opinion/articles/2011/08/adult-manifestations-of-childhood-sexual-abuse.

Alturalearning.com. "Positive Impact: Why Grandparents are Key to Children's Development." *Altura Learning.* March 14, 2017. Accessed August 2020.

Burns, Bob and Whiteman, Tom. *The Fresh Start Divorce Recovery Workbook: A step-by-step program for those who are divorced or separated.* Nashville, TN: Thomas Nelson, Inc., 1992.

Chapman, Gary. *The 5 Love Languages.* Accessed July 2020. https://www.5lovelanguages.com/.

Jeglic, Elizabeth. "What Parents Need to Know About Sexual Grooming: Understanding the stages of sexual grooming can help to protect your child." *Psychology Today.* Assessed September 2020. https://www.psychologytoday.com/us/blog/protecting-children-sexual-abuse/201901/what-parents-need-know-about-sexual-grooming.

NCSBY.org. "Normative Sexual Behavior." *National Center on the Sexual Behavior of Youth.* Assessed September 2020. http://www.ncsby.org/content/normative-sexual-behavior.

NIDA. "What is Cocaine?." *National Institute on Drug Abuse,* 20 Jul. 2020, https://www.drugabuse.gov/publications/research-reports/cocaine/what-cocaine.

Psychiatry.org. "What is Intellectual Disability?" *The American Psychiatric Association.* Accessed October 2020. APA_DSM-5-Intellectual-Disability.pdf, 2013.

Rehabs.com. "Addiction is a Family Disease and Possible Treatment Options." *American Addiction Center.* Accessed August 2020. National Rehabs Directory. https://www.rehabs.com/addiction/family-disease/.

UKY.EDU. *University of Kentucky College of Arts & Sciences: Mathematics.* Accessed September 2020. www.math.as.uky.edu.

RESOURCES

Child Help National Child Abuse Hotline

https://www.childhelp.org/childhelp-hotline/

1-800-4-A-Child or 1-800-422-4453

Child Welfare Information Gateway

https://www.childwelfare.gov/pubs/reslist/tollfree/

One Parent Scholar House | Formerly known as Virginia Place
(Lexington, Kentucky)

https://oneparentscholarhouse.org

1-859-252-4828

Substance Abuse and Mental Health Services Administration

https://www.samhsa.gov/find-help/national-helpline

1-800-662-4357

www.ingramcontent.com/pod-product-compliance
Lightning Source LLC
Chambersburg PA
CBHW051838090426
42736CB00011B/1872